EVERY ADULT'S
GUIDE
— TO —
TALKING TO
TEENS

Kathy Paterson

Pembroke Publishers Limited

© 1995 Pembroke Publishers
538 Hood Road
Markham, Ontario, Canada L3R 3K9

Canadian Cataloguing in Publication Data

Paterson, Kathleen M., 1943–
  Every adult's guide to talking to teens

Includes index.
ISBN 1-55138-061-7

1. Teenagers. 2. Adolescent psychology. I. Title.

EQ796.P37 1995   305.23'5   C95-931401-6

A catalogue record for this book is available from the British Library.
Published in the U.K. by Drake Educational Associates
St. Fagan's Road, Fairwater, Cardiff CF5 3AE

Editor: Joanne Close
Design: John Zehethofer
Cover photography: Ajay Photographics
Typesetting: Jay Tee Graphics Ltd.

This book was produced with the generous assistance of the government of Ontario through the Ministry of Culture and Communications.

Printed and bound in Canada by Webcom
9 8 7 6 5 4 3 2 1

Contents

Introduction *9*

Chapter One: What and Why *11*
Adult Approaches *12*
   The Militant Approach *13*
   The Child-Centred Approach *13*
   The Flexible-Structure Approach *14*
Who Is Responsible? *15*

Chapter Two: Respect *17*
Respecting the Adolescent *18*
Trusting the Adolescent *19*
   Trust Builders *20*
When Trust Is Difficult *22*
   Silence *22*
   Money Matters *22*
   Positive Thinking *23*
   Faith *23*
   Worst Possible Scenario *23*
Adult Belief in Self *24*
Being Fair and Consistent *25*
   Allow Equal Time *26*
   Keep Your Word *26*
   Evaluate Objectively *27*
   Final Words on Respect *27*

Chapter Three: Communicating with Adolescents *28*
More than Listening *29*
The Importance of Timing *30*
Communication Considerations *31*
   Awareness *31*
   Make Time *31*
   Location *31*
   Initiate the Conversation *32*
   The Silent Treatment *32*
   Guide the Conversation *33*

The Adult's Turn *34*
Written Conversations *34*
Constructive Conferences *36*
Non-Verbal Communication *38*
Hugs! The Issue *39*
The Role Model *40*
Giving Advice *42*

Chapter Four: Prevention and Enforcement *43*
Offensive Tactics *44*
   Appreciation *45*
   Deprivation *47*
   Attitude *47*
   Attention *51*
   Rules *53*
   Goals *57*
   Space *59*
   Reinforcement *60*

Chapter Five: Discipline *65*
Minor Misconduct *66*
Serious Misconduct *66*
Anger *67*
   Time Out *67*
   Arguments *68*
   Ignorance *68*
   Extenuating Circumstances *69*
   The Power Struggle *69*
Rescuing *70*
Accountability *73*
   Accountability at School *74*
   Accountability at Home *75*
Discipline: Natural and Unnatural Consequences *77*
   Natural Consequences *78*
   Automatic Natural Consequences *80*
   Unacceptable Natural Consequences *81*
   Unnatural Consequences *81*
Adolescent Violence *85*
   Possible Reasons for Adolescent Violence *86*
   Dealing with Adolescent Violence *87*

Chapter Six: Topical Issues *90*

About Grades *90*

About Homework *92*

About Apathy *94*
  Look for the Niche *95*
  Reinforce the Insignificant *96*
  Enforce the Physical *96*
  Remain Flexible and Positive *97*
About Independence *97*

About Peers *99*
  When Peers Are a Problem *100*
  Putting Peers to Work for You *101*
About Dating *103*

About Sexuality *105*
  Experimentation *106*
About Privacy *107*

About Money Matters *109*

About Clothes *111*

About Alcohol and Drug Abuse *113*
  Experimentation *114*
  Substance Abuse *114*

A Final Word *116*

Appendix: The Questionnaire *117*

Index *125*

Introduction

A good teacher is always a beginner.
A good parent is always learning.
But,
A good book is only as good as those who read it!

K.P.

Adolescence, as I'm sure no one will argue, is a difficult period marked by physical changes and emotional upheavals. Issues that in earlier years would have been of little consequence – appearance, group identification, and relationships – become major concerns. As adolescents struggle to establish an identity for themselves, they often clash with authority figures – parents and teachers – who they believe stymie their efforts of self-expression and hence self-discovery.

As adults, many of us have (thankfully) forgotten the intense periods of self-doubt, anxiety, and despair that accompany this period of growth. When we attempt to solve an issue that arises with an adolescent, whether it be in the classroom or in the home, we do so from our adult perspective, based on our experiences and our desire to help. What we sometimes forget is that the adolescent also has his or her own perspective that needs to be heard and addressed before the issue at hand can be dealt with effectively.

Through the twenty years I have spent with adolescents in classroom settings and with my own children and their friends, I have come to realize that we need to both recognize and value the unique perspective these young people hold. When we understand how adolescents feel about a situation and the reasons for these feelings, we are better equipped to deal with problematic issues that arise in our daily interactions.

It is because of this need to increase communication that I developed the questionnaire on which sections of this book are based. My goal was to determine adolescents' views and feelings and then collate them with behaviors and responses with which most adults are already familiar. Administered to a group of adolescents aged thirteen to eighteen in an urban working-class area, the questionnaire explored a range of topics, from influences on their life through their attitude toward sex education. Questionnaires could be anonymous, however most participants chose to record their name, providing evidence of the adolescent need to be heard by an adult.

Although no credibility checks were run and this was, by its nature, not a statistically correct survey, it must be said that the general responses reflected my original beliefs of adolescents and how they would like to interact. The suggestions in this book are based largely on what has (and has not) worked for me over the years. Naturally, everyone is different and has his or her own unique way to communicate, to create familiarity, to guide, and to love. I hope the correlation of adolescent views and possible adult actions will provide new insights and help you to confirm that the path you are on is the right one.

This book, based on findings from the questionnaire and from my work with adolescents, will attempt to provide some solutions, or at least some survival tips, for adults who deal with adolescents in both school and home settings. I realize that some of you will disagree with the premises and suggestions I propose, and that is fine. At least the reflection of the concepts will provide food for thought.

It is important to stress that the issues discussed in this book reflect common adolescent behaviors. In instances where an adolescent has serious behavioral or emotional problems, expert help should be sought immediately.

As an aid to encourage dialogue with adolescents, you may use the questionnaire in its entirety or employ specific sections as you see fit. In your hands, the questionnaire can become a tool to open discussion with one or more adolescents in your class or with your child at home.

We know that there is no one answer that will solve all of the difficulties and heartaches involving adolescents today. Two sure ways to fail, however, are to try to please everyone, or to be indifferent. One of the saddest phrases spoken by an adult is, "It might have been different if I had. . . ." Do what you think is necessary. Take one day at a time. Have faith in yourself and in the adolescent. You *will* make a difference.

CHAPTER ONE

What and Why

A teenager is a curious thing,
One moment a glorious breath of spring,
Then all of the fury of winter's chill
Replaces the smile with a look fit to kill.

Without warning the child who is happy at home
Turns into a teen screaming, "Leave me alone!"
Then the teen plays the adult without any fears,
Just "hanging" and "cruising" with adult-like peers.

But no matter what face with true adults they share
One thing is certain – they want them to care!
To be patient and wait 'till the turmoil is through
They may never show it but teens need love too!

K.P.

This decade seems to have brought with it a new epidemic of adolescent unrest, much of which is reported in detail by all facets of the media. Edgar Z. Friedenberg, author of *The Vanishing Adolescent*, stated as early as 1959 that the adolescent seemed to have replaced the communist as the appropriate target for public controversy and foreboding. In truth, given the current conditions of adolescent disenchantment with the world, one can't help but be concerned about the future of our youth. Is there a solution to the problems they represent and the problems they face? Can we deal with these young people in such a manner that they will, in fact, become productive, responsible and caring individuals? Is there hope for tomorrow?

"Yes! Yes! and Yes again!" It is time to reassess the way in which we, as adults, too often view people between the ages of thirteen and nineteen, and see instead the wonderful integrity of their existence. Adolescents today are the products of the society we have created and are therefore the responsibility, not the burden, of that society. There are no magic answers or instant cures, but there are the voices of the young to guide us. Consider the following conversation, quoted as heard.

ADULT: What is it that adolescents want? Do you want total freedom to do as you choose?

ADOLESCENT: No! Of course not!

ADULT: But you refuse to accept the established rules.

ADOLESCENT: That's because they're dumb! There are too many and they don't let me breathe.

ADULT: If I remember correctly, we set those rules together. You agreed that you needed structure.

ADOLESCENT: I know, and I do. It's just that there has to be some, you know, flexibility in the structure. Like, do you always follow every rule exactly? Aren't there. . . different circumstances or something?

Flexibility in the structure – a concept that, at least initially, appears to be a contradiction of terms. This adolescent's opinion, however, is not an isolated one. The majority of his counterparts lean toward the necessity of structure (rules), but within the guidelines of flexibility and fairness. They accept the necessity of consequences, and most admit that they would not leave school (contrary to what they say aloud) because they could not take care of themselves. What they strenuously object to are rules that do not allow them freedom of choice or room to move. Thus it becomes necessary to consider the best adult approach within a framework of what adolescents believe to be fair.

Adult Approaches

There appear to be two distinct and relatively incompatible approaches used in dealing with adolescents. The first is what I will refer to as the Militant Approach; the second, the Child-Centred Approach. Neither approach, unfortunately, will succeed in isolation.

What, then, is one to do? A brief explanation of both approaches will facilitate my answer.

The Militant Approach

This method assumes that the adolescent will only function appropriately within the confines of a rigid structure and controlled atmosphere. In fact, control is the key word here. This applies to both the home and school environment, with consistency being an absolute.

Accountability is maintained through punishment, withdrawal of privileges, and positive reinforcement. Adults are considered more important than adolescents; consequently, they control all situations.

The Child-Centred Approach

This method assumes that the adolescent will only function appropriately when given free rein to explore and express in an atmosphere of acceptance and warmth. Here freedom is the key word with acceptance following closely behind. This approach views structure as a detriment to the development of individuality and creativity. Accountability is maintained through the spontaneous implementation of natural consequences. Adolescents are given unconditional regard and are considered more important than adults.

Obviously I have exaggerated the components of each approach in order to make a point. Current societal problems have forced many naturally child-centred adults to attempt to be militant and vice-versa, without any real idea as to what they are doing. Given that the results are often unsuccessful, I have attempted, with the best interests of adolescents in mind, to create a third approach that combines the strongest points of both Militant and Child-Centred Approaches.

To do this, it was necessary to separate common adult actions and reactions in relation to adolescents into those that usually work and those that usually do not work, based on what young people reported.

DO NOT WORK
- getting involved in a power struggle,
- practising physical abuse, such as corporal punishment,

- setting a poor example (e.g., drinking to excess in presence of adolescents),
- assuming what the adolescent means without asking for clarification,
- setting impossible goals or expectations,
- using put-downs or any other form of emotional abuse,
- enforcing rules without any flexibility,
- utilizing negative reinforcement,
- employing judgmental actions, such as condemnation of the adolescent's peers,
- using threats, warnings, or fear tactics,
- criticizing the adolescent as a human being,
- treating the adolescent like a child,
- withdrawing affection.

DO WORK
- listening and trying to clarify the thoughts/actions/reasons of the adolescent,
- setting as good an example as possible,
- enforcing and sharing accountability fairly,
- trusting and respecting the adolescent,
- using a variety of positive reinforcement,
- being open-minded and non-judgmental,
- being sincere and caring,
- giving of time,
- treating the adolescent as an adolescent, not as an adult or a child,
- appreciating the many merits of adolescence,
- setting clear and reachable goals and expectations,
- being flexible.

The Flexible-Structure Approach

Attributes of the Militant and Child-Centred Approaches overlap when placed in a schematic such as the one shown on the next page. Qualities that overlap become the characteristics of what I have chosen to call the Flexible-Structure Approach.

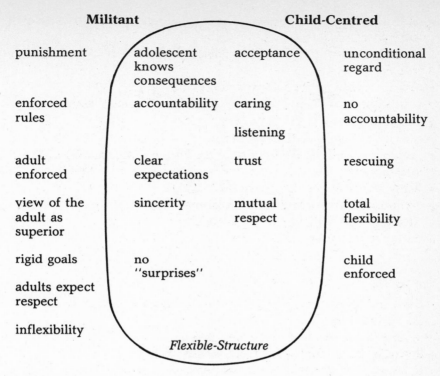

Militant			Child-Centred
punishment	adolescent knows consequences	acceptance	unconditional regard
enforced rules	accountability	caring	no accountability
		listening	
adult enforced	clear expectations	trust	rescuing
view of the adult as superior	sincerity	mutual respect	total flexibility
rigid goals	no "surprises"		child enforced
adults expect respect			
inflexibility			

Flexible-Structure

The Flexible-Structure Approach, then, describes a way of dealing with adolescents that provides them with some necessary structure, but remains flexible and thus more acceptable to them. This, I believe, is what most of us strive for, but as with any guideline it is sometimes easy to lose sight of the goal.

Who Is Responsible?

Now that we have established what we want to do, the next question is, "How is it done?" Questions of how are usually related to explanations of why. In other words, why are we faced with adolescent misbehavior, lack of responsibility and motivation, and absence of respect for others? Teachers will frequently say that the fault lies with the parents. Parents will answer that the school system, hence the teachers, are to blame. Checkmate!

My answer to this question is, "Who cares?" What difference does it make who is responsible for the current crisis? Today's adolescents are the products of our society. The relevant topic is not why, but rather what can be done to rectify the situation and who will accept the responsibility of intervention.

I believe that the future of today's adolescents lies with all of us – parents, teachers, role models, friends, relatives. Placing blame does not solve anything, but taking immediate action might. Far too frequently, I hear adults say, "It is too late to change them when they are teenagers. . . the damage is already done!" I disagree! There is always something a concerned adult can do. I think the difficulty is that many of us do not know what that something is.

Perhaps recalling the fact that we all survived adolescence may have merit. Think back – were you a model teenager? A colleague shared with me some of the horrors of his adolescent years. I was surprised to learn that this industrious, caring, well-loved teacher was once a member of a rough gang. He had taken part in a number of criminal activities, including stealing, vandalism, and attacking and beating others. Today he is a role model for youth. How did this metamorphosis take place? He says simply, "I grew up!" Perhaps time is all it takes! Perhaps we must simply assist our adolescents to survive these years of turmoil with minimum cost to all. With this as our goal, we need to select an approach for dealing with adolescents that allows all of us the freedom to be – safely! This is the premise upon which this book is based. Let us always be open to the miracle of a second chance!

CHAPTER TWO

Respect

"Don't laugh at youth for his affectations;
he's only trying on one face after another
till he finds his own."

Logan Pearsall Smith

"Respect," a young man answered during an adolescent-adult conversation, "is not just being told you are respected. You know, when someone says, 'I respect you for that' usually they don't mean it. Respect is something someone does, in a way that you can't really describe that makes you feel important to them. You know they consider you a worthwhile person even if you do something dumb."

Respect is a key issue to all adolescents, and most do not feel that they get their fair share of it from the adult population. Only select adults gain their respect, but those that do appear to have considerable influence over them. Adolescents tend to agree on those adult actions and behaviors that allow them to feel respected, as well as those adult behaviors that are worthy of respect.

There are no general categories of adults whom adolescents feel offer them respect, although most adolescents cite specific peers and parents. With regard to the questionnaire, it is interesting to note that "adults in general" fell well below the rest of the categories.

Adolescents believe adults most often show respect for them by:

- sharing worries and concerns,
- being honest and trusting the adolescent's honesty,
- talking and listening to them as equals,
- being good role models,
- giving unsupervised responsibilities.

In order to be respected by adolescents, adults must:

- respect the adolescent,
- be "laid back," relaxed,
- be sincere and honest,
- be fair and consistent,
- give adolescents a chance. . . trust them,
- believe in what they are doing – have self-confidence.

Adolescents have definite ideas about what qualities elicit respect, of how respect is shown, and specifically, of their own overwhelming need for respect. Based on these conclusions, I have attempted to provide insight into how adolescents and adults can develop mutual respect through exploration of these issues:

- respecting the adolescent,
- trusting the adolescent,
- when trust is difficult,
- adult belief in self,
- being fair and consistent.

Respecting the Adolescent

The assumption is that an adolescent will respect an adult who first shows him or her respect. This predictable coincidence is one of those magical things about life: when the student is ready, the teacher appears.

This does not vary with the ages of the persons involved. When I was young, a wonderful elderly gentleman told me he had great respect for my integrity. Although at the time I didn't understand what integrity was, I was impressed that such a person could respect me, a mere child. I never forgot that and now that I understand the compliment, I cherish it even more.

Never think that young people are unaware or undeserving of respect. In fact, when it comes to adolescents, this is often uppermost on their minds. A truism that I hear all too often from upset adolescents goes something like, "How can they expect us to respect them, when they have no respect for us?" The question remains: How does one show an adolescent respect, in such a way that she or he recognizes and accepts it as genuine?

18

Trusting the Adolescent

The answer lies in the words trust and faith. Some of you may think that we can't trust adolescents because they might lie. It can be said that we all tell lies, which we often refer to as white lies. By whatever term we call them, they are lies. Adolescents may well be the age group that tells the fewest lies since it is in their nature to be direct. They admire honesty because they want to believe in the goodness of mankind and are not yet as suspicious nor as cynical as adults. They want the truth, and they want to give the truth as they see it. If we can trust them enough to allow them to speak honestly, without fear of judgment or condemnation, most adolescents will be truthful even when they are in the wrong and will be punished for their admissions. If mutual respect has been established, in most cases the youth will be honest.

We must remember that one is "innocent until proven guilty" and give adolescents the benefit of the doubt, at least until we find reason to do otherwise (see p. 22). If the adolescent has lied, then the situation changes. Our tendency to be suspicious of adolescents causes lack of trust, which in turn leads to lack of respect.

It is my opinion that we are suspicious because we are concerned about what might go wrong and consequently cause pain to adolescents and, ultimately, to ourselves. As parents, there is the very real fear for the safety of our children. We remember our own adolescent crises; we want to protect our children from harm at all costs. Consequently, we behave too often in ways that the adolescent sees as foolish, overprotective, or unnecessary. The adolescent feels a lack of trust and respect, and does not appreciate the fact that the grown-up desire for safety, and hence security, overpowers the respect for the adolescent that otherwise might be there.

So what is the answer? Be flexible. Don't create problems in advance. If the job of parenting and teaching has been done in the early years, the message may well be imprinted. If it hasn't, last-minute cautions will have little effect. The best you can do is to trust the adolescent and recognize this as an instance over which you have almost no control. Adult flexibility in this case comes from showing trust and confidence in him or her, and in the constancy of your faith in and support of the adolescent.

There are many ways in which we can work toward the establishment of trust between ourselves and an adolescent. Here are some examples that came out of a brainstorming session I held with a group of adolescents.

Trust Builders

- Be real with your emotions. Share them with the adolescent. Accept suggestions openly. If you are upset about something, tell the adolescent. It is not necessary to explain why you are unhappy. The youth will not probe, and will feel important because you have shared this information with him or her. As a teacher, I have never been good at hiding my emotions from my students. First, adolescents are aware of any sign of emotion. Second, I tend to "wear my heart on my sleeve." My students have always been supportive. As an example, when I was in the midst of experiencing a long "low," three sixteen-year-old students took it upon themselves to escort me between classes for a day, all the while filling my head with ridiculous jokes and "what ifs?" I defy anyone to remain serious in such conditions.
- Share some of your life with the adolescent. This is especially important if the adolescent is experiencing some sort of difficulty. Relating a similar incident from your life will help to create a bond of trust.
- Ask the adolescent for help, not with intimate personal problems, but with other real problems. As an example, ask his or her suggestions on what to wear to a certain event, or on the best garage to replace a car muffler. Keep in mind that adolescents are open and real. If she or he tells you that a particular color "is horrible" on you, do not be offended. Instead, be pleased that the adolescent trusts you enough to be frank.
- Share something minor with the adolescent and ask that she or he keep it a secret. Adolescents can be tight-lipped when they see that you trust them. That said, the adolescent population mirrors its adult counterpart: some people are incapable of keeping a secret. Be prepared for the rumor mill, and don't share something that will cause harm should this occur.
- Ask for help that involves faith in the adolescent. A teacher can ask for help with after-school activities. A parent can ask

for assistance with more personal activities such as helping to plan a special celebration.

- Provide for some adult-like responsibilities that the adolescent can assume. Here are some examples:

AT SCHOOL

- keeping attendance,
- setting up a lab,
- being the doorperson (students who find it difficult to remain in the room often make the best doorpersons),
- making phone calls for you,
- being in charge of collecting money for class or school activities,
- retrieving something from your car. I have discovered this to be a big thing for younger adolescents, who assume the responsibility with pride and dependability. I once asked a young man, known to be light-fingered, to do this task. In my car were many easily lifted items such as tapes. I am happy to report that nothing, other than the requested item, was touched. Trust!

AT HOME

- dealing with repairmen (e.g., phoning, paying). As well as establishing trust, this teaches the adolescent about the cost of living.
- sharing duties. This means discussing with the adolescent what needs to be done, then sharing these duties on a daily basis. As an example, rather than assuming that the adolescent will always baby-sit on demand, agree to specific nights that suit everyone.
- if a daughter or son drives the family car, she or he can share the responsibility of maintenance. Work out a budget, and let the adolescent assume responsibility for cleaning, general maintenance, and so on.

When you ask for assistance from an adolescent, follow up with reinforcement. Again, this constitutes the structure component of the Flexible-Structure Approach. If you request help from a peer, you would offer retribution. This situation is the same. Think respect! Payment will, of course, vary with the situation.

A final word about trust. Three words that breed lack of trust – insecurity, inconsistency, and inaccessibility – should be remembered by all of us.

When Trust Is Difficult

Of course there will be times when it is difficult to trust the adolescent. These are the times when you, as the adult, must have faith and trust, not only in the adolescent, but also in yourself. You need to feel confident that you can handle the situation in a flexible yet structured manner. The following examples may be familiar to you.

Silence

When an adolescent's silence shuts you out, trust him or her to deal with it alone. Each adolescent needs solitude, and the more an adult attempts to infringe upon this, the less respect she or he will receive. If you must say something, a simple phrase such as, "I can see you need to be alone. I'll be _____ if you need me" is sufficient.

Money Matters

When you give an adolescent money for a specific purchase and expect change, trust that you will receive the correct change without giving a lecture. An acquaintance shared with me the following experience. She had given her son, Neil, a fairly large sum of money so he could buy a pair of shoes. When Neil returned the change but no receipt, she became suspicious. Although she had no reason to disbelieve him, she "checked up" on Neil by visiting the store where he had bought the shoes. To her delight (she admitted to being glad to have "finally" caught him at being dishonest), the shoes were there, less $20.00 of the price that Neil reported. The original price was what he had quoted to her, but the shoes were on sale. Proud of herself, she confronted Neil who was mortified. After insisting he had paid full price for the shoes, he refused to talk to her. Some time later, Neil found the crumpled receipt in the pocket of his jeans. He had not lied. Needless to say, Neil's mother was humiliated and remorseful, but the damage was done. Given that adolescents tend to be more forgiving than adults, it is likely that Neil forgave his mother. That said, their level of mutual respect was greatly affected by the incident.

Positive Thinking

When an adolescent does something for the first time (e.g., takes the car alone, goes camping without adult supervision, goes on a first date), trust that nothing untoward will happen. In an instance such as this, flexibility on your part is paramount. Instead of lecturing and nagging about the possible difficulties that may arise, wish the adolescent well. Focus, for both of you, on the exciting positives of this venture, and be happy for the adolescent. It is your responsibility to set a few guidelines, such as when to be home, but the more words you waste on expounding negatives, the less trust, and therefore respect, you show the adolescent.

Faith

When there is a gathering where you know there will be temptations, such as an unchaperoned house party, realize that you cannot protect the adolescent forever and that she or he will be fine. Your faith in the adolescent will go a lot farther than suspicions, and will build a healthy structure of pride in which your child can function.

Worst Possible Scenario

In instances where you can't stop worrying about possible negative outcomes, thinking of worst possible scenarios may help. In the example above, think of the worst possible thing that could happen (e.g., your child got stoned and arrested). Could you cope with this? Realize that you could, and that the world would remain largely unchanged. As a rule, adults fantasize the most improbable happenings, but realize that even these situations can be faced if necessary. By some unknown rationale, this imagining of the "worst" gives most of us a sense of calm and control, allowing us to trust the adolescent more readily. It is probably best to keep these "worst possible scenarios" to yourself: if they are shared with an adolescent, they illustrate neither trust nor respect.

In the end, respect involves having faith in these exciting young people. When it is the right time, they will get it together and grow up in spite of us. Be prepared to give them a chance, and another chance when they mess up the first time. This is flexibility! Trust them and they will become trustworthy. Be honest with them, and they will be honest in return. This is structure!

Adult Belief in Self

Adolescents respect those adults who have confidence in themselves and are secure in what they do. Statements such as the following from junior high students give evidence of this fact:

- Mr. M. is a great science teacher because he knows so much and makes it all seem really important.
- Mrs. S. is a super mum. She has great taste in clothes and wears her hair in a cool style, but not like a kid. Do you know what I mean?
- I like Mr. T. because he doesn't talk a lot, but when he does it's always about important stuff.
- If I need help, I go to Mrs. F. because she's a good listener and doesn't get mad when I say bad things.
- Mrs. L. really makes me believe that school is important, even when I don't think so.
- I like Ms. W. because she is cool and sort of strict, but she likes us and she stands up for us.
- Mr. C. works real hard and I admire that because it makes me want to work hard too and not be lazy like I am.
- Mrs. K. is neat. She has all those kids but she never gets freaked out and she works at a hard job to keep her kids fed and stuff. And she doesn't drink or smoke because she can't afford to I guess. And she always smiles. I like that.

Obviously these adults believe in themselves, have positive self-esteem, and by nature, are relatively relaxed. But what if this isn't the case? What if you, like many of us today, are so burdened with the reality of daily existence that you do not have the time or the energy to build a healthy self-image? The best suggestion I can make is to be as honest as possible with the adolescents with whom you are involved. Adolescents appreciate adult concerns, responsibilities, anxieties, and even subsequent periods of depression, as long as the situation is shared with them to some degree. In these instances, honesty helps. Explain that you are responsible for your current situation, just as they are responsible for theirs. Sometimes a discussion about what you have (or should have) learned is useful. The discussion provides a sense of structure for the adolescent, allows him or her to participate in your potential learning situation, and makes him or her feel trusted and respected.

It is important for us to present positive values and moral standards for adolescents. Avoid use of the "do as say but not as I do" rule since adolescents see the rule for what it is (or isn't). While they are forgiving and accepting, they tend to respect those who believe in themselves and are not afraid to make a statement. The irony is that if the adult is confident, the ability to be humorous and relaxed will come naturally.

I was somewhat surprised by the importance adolescents attached to an adult's faith, not only in himself or herself, but also in what the adult does. The adult who works as an accountant, for example, but disparages of his or her occupation is viewed less highly by adolescents than the adult who performs a lower-status job, but is proud of his or her work and does it well. Similarly, the teacher who instructs in a lackadaisical manner with no apparent commitment to the material being taught is seldom respected by adolescents, despite the lighter student work-load that usually accompanies this attitude. Adults who constantly second-guess themselves, procrastinate, or are apathetic elicit little adolescent respect.

What can you do? Begin with a critical self-examination. Are you guilty of one or more of these attitudes? If yes, think about altering your attitude. Make yourself accountable to yourself. Start by becoming aware of who you are and what you believe in then let the rest of the world in on this information. Belief in one's self begins with an appreciation of life, and a knowledge that you can make a difference!

Being Fair and Consistent

Nobody likes a "pet," be it a teacher's pet or a parent's pet. The adult that allows himself or herself to be caught in this situation will surely lose the respect of other adolescents, and possibly even that of the preferred youth. This is not to say that we can't and won't have favorites since it is human nature to prefer some persons more than others. That said, we must have the maturity to prevent the situation from becoming problematic. If you feel closer to some adolescents than to others, remember to allow the preferred youths space. Don't allow your feelings to smother the adolescent and/or ostracize others. Think structure here, and realize that you must be flexible with your attention within a framework that allows equality for all.

Fairness, and more importantly, consistent fairness, is a priority with adolescents of all ages. They have respect for those adults who they deem to be impartial, and who can be relied upon to behave in a predictable manner most of the time. As with many of the situations described in this book, this behavior is easier said than done – awareness is the first step. There are, however, a few suggestions that may help you to be more successful in this area.

Allow Equal Time

Whether this is time divided between two siblings or thirty students, time-sharing is mandatory. As teachers, we always seems to spend the most time with the best or worst students. If you are a teacher, be aware of this and make it one of your goals to spend equal time with those "middle" students who work quietly on their own. In the inside jacket of my plan book, I have written the names of the students in this group. I try to talk with at least one or two or these students each day, placing a mark beside the names of those I have spoken with so that I don't overlook anyone. This equal time is every bit as important in the home.

Keep Your Word

In fairness to everyone, we must try to keep promises to adolescents. Breaking a promise, even to a peer, should be avoided, however we have the maturity plus the experience to at least understand. The adolescent has neither, and thus views the broken word as unfair and inconsistent. Don't promise something that you can't uphold. If you have to withdraw from the commitment, offer a truthful and sincere apology.

Evaluate Objectively

This may well be one of the most difficult issues for adults. How many of us are guilty of comparing one sibling's or one student's behavior with that of another? Each person is an individual, and never more so than in adolescence. In their own words, "they hate being compared!" I realize that it is impossible to always avoid this predicament, but at least we should be aware of it and aim for consistency and some degree of structure.

Final Words on Respect

The issue of mutual respect is crucial. In keeping within the confines of the Flexible-Structure Approach, it can be said that it is the responsibility of the adult to remain flexible in bestowing respect for the adolescent, thereby creating a structure of trust and honor. Adolescents cannot do this for themselves. They crave respect, but don't have the experience and/or maturity to understand the subtleties of the issue. The adult, then, must respect each adolescent for what she or he is, and assist with the development of further respectable behavior by serving as a role model. The suggestions in this chapter will, hopefully, make this important task more surmountable.

> You're never too old to hug or to hold. . .
> You're never too young to respect!
> You're never too grand to be given a hand. . .
> And there's NEVER a time for neglect!
>
> *K.P.*

CHAPTER THREE

Communicating with Adolescents

> "To use the same words is not sufficient guarantee of understanding: one must use the same words for the same genus of inward experience. Ultimately one must have one's experiences in common."
>
> *Friedrich Nietzsche*

Adolescents have firm ideas about what constitutes a good conversation so it is to our advantage to discover what it is adolescents value. Words alone are not enough.

In order to gain further insight into the adolescent-adult communication process, I asked adolescents at my school to form discussion groups. The topic of the discussion was factors that increase positive adolescent-adult communication. The groups came up with the following list of recommendations for adults to consider when talking to adolescents.

DO
- maintain eye contact,
- give the adolescent your full attention,
- provide suggestions, but allow the adolescent to choose the topic,
- remain positive and calm, but be honest with emotions (e.g., don't say, "It doesn't matter" when it does).

DO NOT
- say, "When I was your age. . . ,"
- say, on a constant basis, "What do you think?"

- pretend to know everything,
- sigh, cry constantly, or act disgusted,
- give ultimatums,
- try to use "in" words in order to be accepted by adolescents.

When adolescents were asked what makes them listen to some adults and not to others, they gave responses that were easy to summarize. In order of importance, adolescents listen to an adult who:

- listens to them first,
- talks to them like an adult more than a child – doesn't yell, nag, or lecture,
- can be trusted to keep secrets and/or give honest answers,
- is a caring person,
- uses words they understand.

More than Listening

With Nietzsche's quote in mind, I would add that when the two parties are adults and adolescents, the chance of understanding is even less than in other mixed pairs. Indeed, there is much more to communicating with adolescents than merely listening and offering advice. The language we use may consist of the same words, but the meanings of the words may vary according to the age group using them. This leads, of course, to misinterpretation and misunderstanding. One of the biggest complaints I hear from adolescents is that "adults don't understand." I have decided that we really do not understand, and therefore make incorrect assumptions. To illustrate this point, I would like to share with you the following story.

Each morning, Keri would hang around my desk and make a nuisance of herself. When I would ask her what she wanted, she would reply, "You don't understand!" Since I was always busy and she was annoying, I would respond with some feeble attempt at humor such as, "Well now is not the time for confessions, so please sit down." This interaction was becoming a ritual until I decided to try to understand what was going on. I told Keri I wanted to understand, but I needed her help. I asked her to step outside the room so I could give her my full attention and encouraged her to talk. She did – it was like water bursting over a dam. What Keri said was, "Ms. P., every morning I go through all my clothes and I can never find the right thing to wear so I change a whole bunch of times and then miss my bus and I still don't have the right clothes and so I have to cover up with this huge shirt and now I'm going to be too hot all day!" My first instinct was to laugh, but this was no laughing matter to Keri. We worked out a solution to her problem with the help of her foster mother. The "desk-hanging" stopped, but what is more important is the lesson I learned. Deal with adolescents now, not later, and always be alert to what their behavior, as well as their words, communicates.

The Importance of Timing

ADULT: Okay, here I am. Let's talk.

ADOLESCENT: I don't feel like talking.

ADULT: But you said you wanted to talk to me.

ADOLESCENT: That was before.

ADULT: Honestly! I don't understand you.

ADOLESCENT: Exactly.

This mother-daughter conversation will, I'm sure, be a familiar one for many readers. While it is not indicative of a major problem, it does illustrate the effect of bad timing on communication. Possibly the easiest way to remedy the situation is for the adult to say something like, "I'm sorry I wasn't available to talk when you wanted. Can we make it some other time?"

The issue of timing is of prime importance to the adolescent, who tends to exist in the here and now. As adults, we must try to give them the time needed to discuss or explain a situation when they are ready. The adolescent who wants to talk to you now may be silent later. Assuming that the issue is trivial or that it can wait are incorrect suppositions. The only assumption we can make is that "it is time for a talk." Keeping in mind flexible structure, be prepared for even brief conversations at inopportune moments. Naturally, there will be occasions when any form of conversation is impossible. In these instances, it is up to the adult to establish a time and a location for the talk.

Communication Considerations

A prerequisite for communication with adolescents is the establishment of rapport and mutual respect. Without this, communication will be guarded at best. Given that respect has been established, the following suggestions should be considered.

Awareness

Adolescents, like everyone else, give a variety of signals when they need to talk. Since it is often not acceptable for the adolescent to seek adult help, we have to learn to recognize subtle cues the adolescent makes. Here are some to watch for:

- hanging around you more than usual,
- finding excuses to be near you, but not talking,
- writing notes to you,
- displaying unusual emotions or behaviors,
- daydreaming,
- being tardy,
- being agitated,
- giving other physical signals.

Make Time

Once you are aware of the adolescent's desire to communicate, the next move is up to you. Obviously, if anyone requests time to "talk," you can choose whether or not you wish to co-operate. When dealing with adolescents, your choice is often limited to where and when. Ignoring the request or putting it off with a "Sure, later?" will not endear you to the adolescent who, in all likelihood, will not ask you to talk again. Communicating with young people involves being prepared to listen and setting a specific time and place if the present isn't appropriate. It goes without saying that it is a priority to be on time since the adolescent will be there!

Location

As a teacher, I have found that the best time and place for serious talks are "at lunch," usually a casual place such as a hamburger grill, or for more formal students, a family-style restaurant. The one-on-one situation allows for the accomplishment of a great deal in a short time span – the adolescent has the freedom to communicate, his or her self-esteem is usually bolstered, and your relationship benefits. This technique works equally well for parent-child interactions.

A car ride can also serve as a time to talk in private. For adolescents who are particularly uneasy about talking, they may find the temporary lack of eye contact comforting. While this may contradict what has been stated earlier, we must realize that there will be exceptions to every rule: just as there are adults who avoid eye contact so too are there adolescents who prefer to distance themselves when speaking about an emotional subject. As well, some cultures do not encourage eye contact, particularly with those of the opposite sex. It is up to us to try to read the adolescent and determine what will make him or her most comfortable.

Parents have the option of holding discussions in the adolescent's room; teachers can simulate this by finding a quiet office or empty class. In addition, activities such as washing the car, gardening, cleaning a classroom, preparing art and science labs, and walking the dog offer ideal times and places for discussions. Often an activity-related talk such as this will seem less threatening to the adolescent.

Initiate the Conversation

Now that the situation is set, you can begin the conversation with a sincere and non-judgmental sentence, such as "You look like you need to talk" or "What's up? You look angry." All of these openers suggest your availability for discussion; they leave the content and the choice of whether to talk or not up to the adolescent.

The Silent Treatment

If the adolescent becomes silent, which is often the case, do not press the issue. The next step is up to the adolescent, and no amount of prompting or questioning will make him or her open up, even though she or he initiated the communication process. If, after several minutes, the adolescent is still silent, it is best to suggest another meeting using statements such as, "Sometimes I don't feel like talking either. That's okay. Why don't you think about it and we can sit down again on _____ at _____. Is that time okay with you?" or "I think you want to be alone right now. That's fine with me. I'll be _____ if you change your mind."

Don't think of this situation as time lost – you have established a bond of trust and a caring structure that might encourage the adolescent to seek you out when she or he is more communicative. You may try to interpret the reason for the non-communication but this is typically a waste of time. As a rule, you will misinterpret what is going on if you attempt to force answers from a mute adolescent. A young girl once said to me in such a situation, "Just let it go!" This is good advice.

Guide the Conversation

The following list, while it may seem somewhat simplistic, details qualities that adolescents look for in a conversation with an adult:

- emotional stability,
- eye contact,
- as few interruptions as possible,
- physical reassurance such as patting the adolescent's hand or arm (this should occur only in relationships where there is a history of this style of rapport),
- non-presumptuousness,
- patience,
- confidentiality,*
- open-mindedness,
- honesty regarding emotions,
- expression of genuine feelings,
- ability to deal with the situation in the present (long-range plans or actions can be discussed later),
- ability to view the individual and situation as unique (e.g., avoid making generalizations and comparisons),
- sincerity,
- non-judgmental words or actions,
- conversation wrap-up and, if necessary, plans to meet again.

* If you think you may not be able to listen in confidence, tell the adolescent immediately. Allow him or her to decide whether

to continue. If she or he chooses to stop the conversation, don't leave the adolescent in the lurch. If possible, provide the name of another person with whom she or he could speak. If the adolescent has been abused, you are required by law to report this. In this case, tell him or her what you have to do, and assure the adolescent that you will continue to be supportive.

The Adult's Turn

It goes without saying that not all discussions are instigated by an adolescent. Often, a concerned adult will want to broach a topic with an adolescent. In these instances, the same rules of adolescent-adult communication apply. I have taped a summary of the following rules to the inside of my desk drawer as a helpful reminder. If you are a teacher, you can do the same: if you are a parent, you can keep a summary at home in a convenient location.

1. Be aware of need.
2. Provide a time and place for discussion.
3. Open and encourage talk.
4. Practise non-judgmental acceptance of silence.
5. Use good communication skills.
6. Find a solution, even if it is only temporary.
7. Close discussion.

Written Conversations

As I'm sure most teachers have noticed, adolescents like to "write notes" and pass them back and forth while the teacher pretends not to notice. This activity can bring about what I call "an infringement of privacy" when a teacher feels obligated not only to take the note from the adolescent, but to also read its contents. The adolescent should not write notes in class, but such retaliatory action on the part of the teacher only serves to embarrass and/or alienate the adolescent. There are better ways to handle such a situation. Here are a few examples that allow for both the protection of the adolescent's shaky self-esteem and the teacher's expression of dislike for breaking rules.

1. Confiscate and destroy the note. Ask the violator to see you _____ (specify).

2. Ask the violator to get rid of the note and to see you _____ to discuss why this is an inappropriate behavior.

3. Tell the class (or group) that you are aware of the "postal express" in the room and that you will provide twenty seconds for it to end or _____ (consequence).

Give the adolescent the respect you would expect if someone accidentally read some of your correspondence. (Think back to a time when someone opened a letter addressed to you, and how you felt at that time.) Both parties can come out of this minor misdemeanor unscathed if the adult acts as an adult.

The notion of note writing has often been overlooked as a viable method of reaching adolescents. I happened upon this technique quite by accident when I found, at the bottom of my overflowing mailbox, a note scribbled on the back of a late slip.

thank you for givin me that hug yesterday it mademe feel good luv Yvonne

I recalled the situation. An introverted young girl been standing alone after the last bell. I approached her, but soon realized that this was one of those times that the adolescent didn't want to talk. I reminded her where she could find me later if she wanted to, and gave her a little hug before I left. I thought nothing more of it, and was not surprised when Yvonne did not seek me out. Obviously, though, Yvonne thought more of the incident – her way of expressing appreciation to me was through her note, which she placed in my mailbox.

This was the beginning. Note writing in the form of friendly letters (practising language arts skills at the same time), became an integral part of my teaching. At least once a month, I asked students to write me a confidential letter or note in which they could express their feelings and concerns on a topic of their choice. The notes were not graded. Once I had received all of their notes, I wrote each student a confidential response in return. It wasn't long before students were writing to me on their own time. This form of communication seemed to be enlightening for all. Adolescents, many of whom could never have been able to verbalize their concerns, were able to express themselves on paper and receive an answer (of sorts) in return. Naturally, not all students wrote serious letters all the time, but even the funny notes were an enjoyable communication. As would be expected, some of the problems shared with me required verbal discussions. In these cases, I introduced the idea of meeting by way of a letter.

One parent started this letter-writing activity with his son. The parent first left a letter on his son's bed, along with a piece of blank paper and a pencil. The letter expressed a concern the father had about his son. A few days later, the father found a note on his pillow and so the communication began. The son is in his twenties now, and they still communicate by notes even though they see each other regularly and have long, intimate discussions. The point is, it works!

Constructive Conferences

Similar to the idea of writing notes, this suggestion for facilitating communication between adolescents and adults forces specific "talk times" for both parties. Once a week (or varied according to your needs), determine a time and place for a conference. At this conference, both you and the adolescent will give a positive comment to each other, as well as raise an area of concern. (Avoid remarks based on physical appearance; there is nothing that can be done about this unless it relates to hygiene.) Together, decide what changes are possible. The following examples, one between a teacher and a seventeen-year-old student and the other between a parent and a fifteen-year-old son, illustrate how these conferences can work.

STUDENT: I like the way you gave us extra class time for that assignment, but I don't like the way you mark our assignments. It's not fair.

TEACHER: Why is it not fair and how do you think I could remedy this?

Discussion continues on this topic.

TEACHER: Are you satisfied with that solution?

Student nods.

TEACHER: OK. I really appreciate your openness and willingness to take part in class discussions. You always have lots to say. What concerns me is the fact that you never bring your materials to class.

Discussion and resolutions.

PARENT: I am really glad that you have been coming home at curfew. I know that must be hard sometimes. What I want to discuss with you is the fact that I think you are smoking.

SON: I am not! What makes you think that?

PARENT: Your uncle saw you. I'm not angry, just worried. Can we talk about it?

Discussion on topic.

SON: What really bugs me is that you don't get home when you are supposed to. You make me phone you if I am going to be late, but you never phone me.

Discussion and resolutions.

This technique works well provided that both parties are willing to accept constructive criticism, and not feel wounded or threatened by the concerns of the other. Frequently it is the adult, not the adolescent, who feels the most hurt or annoyance in these encounters. It is important to remember that most adolescents are candid, and don't couch phrases in the way of most adults. Be prepared, then, to receive some truths that may not be pleasant.

Cancelling a conference constitutes a breach in the structure aspect of the model. There are always issues to discuss, even if they are continuations of suggestions from a previous conference. The fact that the conference time and date is set forces both parties to think about their own and the other person's behavior.

This type of conference also works in a school environment, although finding a time for meeting with all students can be difficult. Results, however, are well worth the effort. There is a saying that "youth and age will never agree." Constructive conference situations often disprove this adage.

Relating these methods of communication to the Flexible-Structure Approach is not difficult. Flexibility is evident in the non-judgmental, open-minded responses, and in the willingness to listen sincerely, consider options, appreciate the adolescent's point of view, and allow for silence. The structure component is suggested by the adult's insistence on structured talks (e.g., writing letters, having lunches, holding conferences), expectations that the adolescent will co-operate within this framework, and mutual compliance with the rules of good discussion.

Non-Verbal Communication

Adolescents are masters at non-verbal communication. Consider the icy looks they cast an adversary, the instant facial changes, the wonderful hand shakes and hand signals, the adolescent walk, not to mention the incredible array of ingenious hair, make-up, and clothing styles they display. Adults often become annoyed by these seemingly blatant rebuttals of society, instead of viewing them as expert forms of non-verbal communication. What wonderful safe ways to say, "Look at me. I am an individual. I care." Confident adults are more likely to accept these forms of expression with an open mind. Perhaps we all need to remember that these exhibitions of non-verbal communication are not harmful or illegal. To pass judgment on them is not only foolish but also unkind.

Adolescents are equally adept at picking up on non-verbal messages. This means that as adults, we must ensure that our actions match our words. Young children expect adults to be perfect – adolescents are not so naïve. They know we are far from perfect, but usually are willing to forgive us as long as we are sincere. When you say something to an adolescent while masking your true feelings behind a smile or a wink, rest assured that the adolescent will see through the mask. Silence is a better approach if you are unwilling to say what you mean or feel.

There are many non-verbal signs we can give to an adolescent. We are all aware of them, but often overlook or underestimate their worth. Take, for example, the simple wink. Depending on the situation it can mean anything from, "It's our secret" to "I have faith in you." It's an effective non-verbal message that requires little energy on your part.

Obviously smiling and frowning are common non-verbal cues. Keep in mind that a smile works much better than a frown and is less taxing on facial muscles. As well, a sincere smile directed at one adolescent can do more than one hundred frowns. Other forms of effective non-verbal communication are a playful punch, a high-five handshake, a thumbs-up signal (or whatever hand signal is "in" at the time), and a direct look (catching the eye of an individual and openly and honestly acknowledging his or her presence). Adolescents like to be noticed, and this last way is one of the simplest forms of acknowledgment. Add a quick smile, and things are off to a great start. Save a pat on the back for younger children (thirteen and younger).

In summary, when dealing with anyone, but especially with adolescents, be aware of the many forms of non-verbal communication, so that they are neither misused nor misread.

Hugs! The Issue

Science and instinct tell us that one good way to reach the sensitive inner spirit is through physical touch. One of the most important forms of this touch is the hug. This issue has particular significance for teachers who often want to comfort their students, but are afraid that their actions might be misinterpreted. This is a real concern, however, I am so convinced of the merits of the hug that I am willing to go out on a limb and commend them.

Before writing this section, I asked hundreds of adolescents how they felt about hugs. The vast majority offered tremendous support for hugging as a means of emotional support and understanding. Many adolescents made a point of telling me they "couldn't live without them," and that they were necessary for normal growth and development.

A hug is given for a specific reason, and only then if the adult has already determined that this form of communication is acceptable to the adolescent. Usually, the adolescent will provide this information by his or her actions. The hug should be given in the presence of others, and in a friendly, strong manner. The best analogy I can think of is that of a hand-shake. We have all experienced the limp handshake that leaves one feeling like the other party is either disinterested or ill. Similarly, we have all experienced the provocative handshake. The best handshake is the warm, firm, strong shake that is accompanied by a smile and kind words. This is the same as a hug. It can be equally rewarding when experienced between peers, adolescents and adults, same sex and opposite sex partners.

If hugging is an action with which you are uncomfortable, do not incorporate it into your non-verbal communication repertoire – you will find other ways to express the same feelings. On the other hand, if you fit into the "well maybe" category, then consider giving the occasional hug. So often, when dealing with adolescents, we do not know how to help. This may be due in part to the fact that the adolescent cannot identify the current cause of concern. In such cases, a hug may not only be appropriate but also helpful.

I give hugs readily, and have become known for this simple gesture. Often students I barely know will come and ask for a hug. They do not offer a reason and I do not ask. They leave with a "thanks" and I may never know what prompted the need for a hug. Why do I do this when I know the risks involved? Because I believe in adolescents, and I believe that no one can ever have too many hugs. Of all age groups, adolescents seem to need hugs the most yet receive them the least. Consider what a hug can say:

I care.
I want to help.
I understand and respect your feelings.
You have my support.
I'm glad to see you.
I will be here for you.
I will share your sorrow/fear/worry.

The Role Model

One of the most obvious yet least considered methods of communicating with adolescents is that of being a role model. All significant adults — relatives, friends or teachers — can be role models. Their actions show clearly their morals and priorities.

With reference to the questionnaire, one of the most common concerns voiced by adolescents centred on adults who smoked, drank, or participated in activities yet at the same time believed they had the right to warn or chastise adolescents about these behaviors. Unlike young children who do not readily make the association between what adults say and do, adolescents are bothered by mixed messages we may send and are aware of even the smallest inconsistencies. A good role model doesn't lead, but rather points the way.

No one expects adults to be paragons of virtue in order that adolescents not be witness to unfavorable behaviors. Rather, the suggestion is that we be aware of what we are doing, when, where, and with whom. The open admission of a weakness is better than appearing deceitful. What we can and must do is be sincere. Sincerity, however, is always subject to proof. It all comes down to "mean what you say; say what you mean." Everything a significant adult does and says is noted by adolescents. Although they may not necessarily mimic behaviors in the way that younger children do, they will evaluate us based on our actions. In fact, sometimes adolescents will behave counter to the witnessed actions. This, too, is a form of learning through communication. Examples of characteristics adolescents seek in a role model include:

- acceptable appearance (e.g., dress code, hygiene, fitness),
- positive work ethics,
- similar interests (e.g., sports, theatre),
- employment of adult behavior, but with a good sense of humor,
- positive self-esteem and outlook on life,
- ability to show love and caring.

As a general rule, we communicate more by what we are than by what we say – non-verbal communication at its most powerful! Think back to your youth. What was there about that one adult – teacher, mentor, relative – that made him or her memorable? I will never forget a no-nonsense teacher who was not afraid to show that she cared for all of us. She had a smile for everyone; she attended all the school functions; and she offered consistent, unconditional support. She was my role model and I had the greatest respect for her.

Being a good role model is not easy, but neither is it impossible. Contrary to the opinion of many, adolescents do not have as their role models movie stars, singers, or other famous or infamous persons. Instead, they select significant adults with whom they have regular contact. We must take pride in these roles, and feel confident about ourselves.

"Nobody holds a good opinion of a man who holds a bad opinion of himself."

Anthony Trollope

Giving Advice

The advice that adolescents report as least useful are those words of wisdom that we believe the adolescent can't do without. These are the same words that we share with them despite the less than enthusiastic response. (No doubt many of us heard these same words of wisdom from our parents.) It is ironic that life can only be understood in hindsight. Where else does advice come from than our own mistakes?

Nevertheless, there are a few suggestions you might want to bear in mind the next time you give advice to an adolescent.

- Keep the words few and the advice simple. Instead of a lengthy dissertation about the perils of drinking and driving, the words, "I suggest you call me (or use this $10.00 for a taxi) if you've been drinking" will be much more powerful.
- Avoid nagging. This is a waste of time. Indicate your respect and trust of the adolescent by the way in which you offer the advice (e.g., "I know that you are mature enough to know when you shouldn't drive, but just in case you don't have enough cash here is $10.00 for cab fare" rather than "You'll probably get too drunk to drive so here's $10.00."
- Remember that advice is only worthwhile if it includes suggestions for the appropriate action(s). The best advice, of course, is a good example that we, based on our experiences and wisdom, are well-equipped to provide.

CHAPTER FOUR

Prevention and Enforcement

"I believe that every right implies responsibility; every opportunity, an obligation; every possession, a duty."
John D. Rockefeller, Jr.

All of us, to a greater or lesser degree, live structured lives. For those of us who work at jobs outside the home, we must meet certain criteria, for example, arriving at work on time, carrying out responsibilities according to written or unwritten rules, and conducting ourselves in a manner that is acceptable to our employers. For those of us who work in alternative situations or at home, we usually experience a greater degree of flexibility in the structure that surrounds us, yet structure remains a vital element of our day. We may have deadlines to meet, obligations to fulfill, or tasks that must be accomplished within a given time period.

Like adults, adolescents need structure, as well as some degree of flexibility within that structure. Structure, when it is fair and rational, provides most people with a degree of comfort and security. Adolescents realize that structure requires enforcement, reinforcement, and, unfortunately, discipline. This chapter will deal largely with that area of enforcement that is primarily preventative, with measures that are proactive rather than reactive and which have been suggested by adolescents.

The adolescent need for structure is apparent in their responses to the questionnaire concerning items related to structure and how it is managed. The following statements provide evidence of this need.

- We like to have freedom to make our own decisions with assistance from adults only if we ask for it. Rules, as long as they aren't stupid, give us some guidelines and excuses for our friends so that we don't have to feel like nerds.

- Discipline for the inappropriate behaviors listed in the questionnaire should be immediate, firm, fair, and consistent. We sometimes do bad things, even though we know they are wrong, just to be part of the group. At times like these, we want some sort of discipline so that we don't feel so guilty.
- Not all kids should be treated the same because there are really bad kids and others who are just experimenting and trying to fit in. The adults should be able to tell the difference.
- We should be given the chance to do stupid things, but not get into trouble for them if we don't hurt anybody but ourselves.

Offensive Tactics

The best defense is a good offense, a well-worn adage and one that is appropriate to the material that follows. As stated earlier, one of the most essential components of healthy adolescent-adult relationships is mutual respect. Within the boundaries of mutual respect, however, both adolescents and adults require limits.

Some adults feel that by taking a firm stand they will alienate the adolescent. Young people generally say "not necessarily so," adding that "it depends on how it is done." Keep in mind issues of trust, fairness, and respect before considering offense, prevention or, at the very least, "readiness." Each of you will apply the suggestions in a unique way – we are all individuals so the number of combinations of personalities and proposals is limitless. The pages that follow deal with concerns of both adolescents and adults in "limit-setting" situations, and offer proven successful suggestions. The material appears under these headings:

- appreciation
- deprivation
- attitude
- attention
- rules
- goals
- space
- reinforcement

Appreciation

Adolescents' need for appreciation is illustrated in their responses when asked what made them happy and unhappy. The majority of adolescents eluded to the desire for positive attention from significant adults. Examples of these answers include:

- I hate it when they only notice when I do something wrong, and never say anything about all the good stuff!
- It makes me happy when my parent or teacher tells me that I am good at something. They never come to see me at sports and that makes me unhappy because I'm good at them.

As adults, we must appreciate that adolescents are in an uncomfortable developmental period that is unaccompanied by benefits experienced by those in child or adult life stages. They are growing at a rapid rate, and will become accountable adults some day. Of course, a few will never mature fully. We often see these persons as eccentric free spirits who inhabit adult bodies. Although we may frown on their approach to life and subsequent inability to face the responsibilities of maturity, in our hearts we feel twinges of jealousy: the adult who maintains some of the mystery of adolescence is generally a happy soul!

Adolescents are delightful, energetic people who are bestowed with idealism and not enough experience with which to monitor it. They are individualists; they speak with candor and honesty; they are concerned about the planet, humanity, and the underdog; they show courage in support of their beliefs; they see humor in the most mundane of instances; and, although all adults may not agree, they demonstrate unchecked motivation and commitment to issues they deem important. For the most part, their hopes and dreams of childhood are still alive, although they may not readily share them with adults. Finally, adolescents crave the novel; they are bored by the repetition adults seek.

Of course they are difficult. Anyone attempting to make sense of his or her own view of life and that of adults is bound to be difficult! As adults, with years of experience and maturity, we must assume the responsibility of beginning any interaction with adolescents with a clear image of who and what they are. I believe that the human being is at its best between the years of thirteen and nineteen. While it is not necessary for you to agree, it is necessary for you to keep an open mind and at least consider some of the positive attributes of adolescents.

In addition to appreciating the mystery and complexity of adolescents' good points, the concerned adult must also be alert to the myriad of difficulties they encounter. According to adolescents, their life is like a roller-coaster ride, due in part to hormonal changes that play havoc with their emotions and bodies. They want so much, and are faced with a society that can offer only a little. Confronted with the reality of the future yet filled with natural adolescent hope, they are in a constant state of agitation.

I recently had the experience of assisting an industrious, concerned sixteen-year-old find summer employment. We contacted over one hundred agencies, from fast-food restaurants to "gopher" office jobs. Everywhere the answer was the same: "Sorry. We don't hire anyone under eighteen, or without experience" or "Sorry, not hiring!" I was amazed. When I was that age, finding summer employment was simply a matter of going to the closest convenience store and asking for work. The adolescent, naturally, had to resign himself to the fact that he would not get a job. My response to this situation was one of anger. How can young people gain work experience? What about adolescents who need financial help to get through high school? How can we expect adolescents to be motivated when they know the realities of today's job market? It's not surprising that many adolescents have adopted a "one day at a time" philosophy given the country's economic outlook.

Of course this bleak view varies with location, socio-economic status, and age – some adolescents do find employment, and are faced with the problem of juggling work and school commitments. In most of these cases, however, the work is of a type that only young people desperately needing money will do. For these reasons, I encourage adults to think carefully about adolescents as a whole, to consider their personalities, their importance to the future of civilization, and the anxiety they experience regarding their role in a world that offers little in the way of security and opportunity. There are, and there always have been, young people who are involved in teen violence, truancy, and vandalism. However, I suggest that we look first at the positives, and form judgments and generalizations based on these characteristics and achievements.

46

Deprivation

Another reality that we must appreciate before taking intervention measures is the fact that a number of adolescents have not been exposed to concepts that the general population sees as commonplace. For example, a fourteen-year-old boy surprised me with his ignorance of common matters. Cory did not understand how a parent could have a different last name from a child, or what the meaning of the preface "Ms" was. He truly believed that manners were for wealthy people only, and that in order to be heard, one had to shout louder than the others. He had never been exposed to sex education at home, and had acquired his sketchy knowledge in this area from peers. How many other blanks were in Cory's developmental experiences, and how did they affect his behavior? Frequently, adults saw only the loud, lazy, rude, unmotivated Cory, who sought attention by careless use of sexual terms and innuendoes. I saw this Cory too, but when I looked more deeply, I was able to appreciate Cory for who and what he was, and was also aware of where some of his annoying, inappropriate behaviors originated. I tried to fill in some of the blanks, rather than dealing with Cory as a "behavior problem" first and a person second.

The issue of deprived youths, whether that deprivation be physical, emotional or intellectual, is growing. And it is not necessarily the parents who are to blame. If blame must be cast, today's economic crisis is at fault. Consider the number of single-parent families trying to survive in a relentless state of poverty and societal mistrust, parents who must work two jobs in order to support their family, and social institutions whose efforts to help families are hampered by reduced funding. All of this occurs in a society that too often points the finger of blame on what it views as its marginal members. No group should be marginalized. In the case of adolescents, we must form a positive and real image of each adolescent that takes into account more than one or two specific behaviors.

Attitude

". . . the longer I live, the more I realize the impact of attitude on life. Attitude is more important than the past, than education, than successes, than failures, than circumstances or money. . ."

Charles Swindoll

When asked what made them listen to some adults and not to others, adolescents' most common response was a positive attitude toward youth on the part of the adult. They tended to avoid adults who they thought had "a bad attitude" toward adolescents.

We need to remember that we can control our attitude. I hear rumblings of dissent: "What if I am sick?" What if I haven't had enough sleep?" "What if I just lost my job?" What if, what if, what if? You can't change these factors, but you can control your reactions, hence, your attitude toward them and to life in general. The word attitude, like the word respect, has been used to excess. How often have you heard or used any of the following expressions?

- I do/don't like your attitude.
- He has a very positive/negative attitude.
- You will have to change your attitude.
- What kind of attitude is that?

Like a number of adults, I adopted these pat phrases with ease. It wasn't until Sandra, an alert thirteen-year-old, followed one of these statements with, "What does that mean? How do I change my attitude?" that I realized just how amorphous the term was. An attitude is a state of mind, which is a personal and intimate matter that is purely subjective and hence not measurable. Given this, what right does a person have to demand that another change his or her private thoughts and consequent behaviors? None at all! What we can do, however, is provide ourselves and others, especially adolescents, with ways of coping with a problematic attitude so that the self and others may react positively instead of negatively. We all know how we can be affected by the attitudes of others. How often have you arrived at a destination, happy to be there, only to be greeted by an angry or upset peer or spouse? For some uncanny reason, the negative attitude overpowers the positive, and frequently you too are soon upset.

The development of a positive attitude is an important aspect of healthy adolescent-adult relationships. I believe one of the most effective ways to develop such an attitude is to learn to recognize your feelings in any situation. If those feelings are negative, yet you have to interact with others, you can portray a more positive attitude by letting some of the tension go and forcing a smile, or at least keeping complaints to yourself for a time. Often, the action of presenting a more positive attitude than what you feel will actually help to lift your mood. This technique, simple though it may seem, should be taught to adolescents who experience tremendous shifts in attitudes as a matter of course.

I'm not suggesting that everyone become a Pollyanna. No one appreciates a perpetual smile, but even less appealing is someone who is always negative. To exert some control over your attitude is evidence of maturity, self-confidence, and flexibility. Similarly, your outward behaviors will remain relatively consistent regardless of your mind state.

The more critical an attitude held by us, the less an adolescent will be co-operative. It is ironic that in our desire to help adolescents be safe and successful we often become critical. What we must realize is that being critical is an attitude, and attitudes can be altered. If we consider how criticism affects us then magnify this ten-fold, we will understand how an adolescent perceives criticism. We need, then, to acquire a non-critical way of communicating. Perhaps it would be helpful to recall our own adolescence, and remember how our attitudes and opinions differed from those of our elders.

"We think our fathers fools, so wise we grow. Our wiser sons, no doubt, will think it so."

Alexander Pope

Criticism is part and parcel of a negative attitude, but it is overshadowed both in intensity and effect by an attitude of indifference. I once asked an adolescent why she looked so sad. When she shrugged her shoulders, I suggested that perhaps someone was angry with her. She stared at me and said, "I wish somebody was. Nobody cares enough about me to even be mad!" Her statement made me aware of the incredible power of indifference. Think back to the last time you received the silent treatment from someone important to you. Faced with this reaction, you become powerless. The common reaction is to seek fault in and blame yourself; the common result is anxiety. Consider the adolescent, with his or her limited experience, in this situation. Unable to decipher the feelings and emotions, confusion and guilt are given their chance to reign supreme. As adults, we must consider the attitude of indifference and its damaging effects, particularly on one who is as vulnerable as an adolescent. If we cannot be positive, then we must try to take a stance of neutrality, but never one of indifference.

The following list of attitude checks, compiled by several grade nine classes for their own use, may be useful for adults. The checks provide some structure to an otherwise flexible issue. The classes involved in this exercise organized the checks into positive and negative indicators of one's attitude.

> "The worst sin toward our fellow creatures is to be indifferent toward them: that's the essence of inhumanity."
>
> *George Bernard Shaw*

AM I
- smiling or showing a neutral face?
- displaying positive body language?
- remaining calm (outwardly at least)?
- prepared to be helpful?
- prepared to be non-judgmental?
- armed with my sense of humor?
- willing to listen as well as to talk?
- prepared to show emotion?
- trying to remain positive?

An issue that needs to be addressed is the way in which adolescents view their attitudes and how they affect themselves and those around them. Adolescents have neither the maturity nor the self-confidence to exert much control over their feelings and their subsequent expression. Consequently, telling them to "change their attitudes" is typically a waste of time. In many cases, the adolescent does not understand the subtleties of the word, even though she or he can verbalize the actions that promote or hinder a positive attitude. When discussing an adolescent's attitude, I have found the following statements to be more successful than reproaches:

- If you keep telling yourself you hate this, then you will. How about trying to stop hating it and just accept it?
- Perhaps you could just smile when you come in and get it over with. Maybe we'd both feel better.
- I don't like the way you speak so negatively about _____; I understand that you dislike _____, but maybe we can find a different way of looking at _____.
- It bothers me when you put down _____. Please keep those thoughts to yourself.

- You always look _____ when you come into this room. Is this how you really feel? If so, what can we do about it?
- When you use that sarcastic tone of voice it makes me uncomfortable and angry. I don't want to feel like that, so how can I help you to stop this?
- The expression on your face when I say it's time to _____ annoys me. Is there something about this activity that you dislike? I would like you to think about why you do this and _____ instead.

It is important to reinforce an adolescent's positive attitude since such acknowledgment improves rapport and heightens your awareness of each other. As a teacher, I have found it helpful to conduct a class on attitudes. We discuss negative attitudes and how they can be altered to make them (and the person) more acceptable to others. It has always been time well spent. A final word about attitude – a flexible approach is mandatory. Adolescents and adults seldom have similar attitudes. The blending of the two is one of those principles that makes life exciting.

"Youth is full of pleasure; age is full of care."
Shakespeare

Attention

What adolescents crave most is attention. Although this may seem a lot like appreciation, it differs in that for the adolescent any kind of attention, even negative attention, is better than none at all. It follows, then, that a good preventative measure would be to provide positive attention before the adolescent is forced to misbehave in order to receive negative attention. Adolescents in need of acknowledgment do not necessarily discriminate between attention for positive or negative behaviors. In both cases, the young person is in the spotlight, exactly where intended.

Adolescents tend to fall into one of three categories: leaders, followers, and loners. Most occupy the middle category. Leaders get a great deal of attention by being the leaders, and often their recognition is enjoyed vicariously by the followers. Loners, although they do not outwardly appear to need attention, may very well be crying for attention through their isolation.

Russ was a good example of a loner. As graduation neared, he calmly announced that he would not be attending. Naturally, his peers began the coaxing ritual. The more they begged Russ to attend, the more he refused. He was getting more attention than he had all year! He even carried it as far as refusing to be a part of the graduation photo. Although he didn't capitulate, Russ was the loser and everyone except Russ seemed to recognize this fact.

We can never give adolescents too much attention. Try to be alert to opportunities where you can provide warm, supportive, and positive attention. We are all familiar with the paradox of the worst-behaved adolescents receiving the most attention while the better-behaved adolescents are ignored. One way in which I have tried to combat this situation is to pay attention to a less demanding adolescent every time a more demanding one has commanded some of my time. A harried parent of an adolescent once asked a psychiatrist, noted for her exceptional dealings with this age group, what simple piece of advice she could give to help her child through those troubled years. The psychiatrist's answer: Be there!

If you are wary of this issue and of the merits of attention in the prevention of negative behaviors, consider adolescents who excel at sports, drama, or academics. They receive considerable attention from adults and peers alike for their talents, and are usually not as entangled in the wide array of attention-getting behaviors illustrated by less achieving peers. On the other hand, consider the average follower. She or he does not stand out in the crowd, but has the same need for recognition. Enter the "look-at-me" behaviors that adults often find disquieting – these are the adolescents who tend to go overboard on "weirdness." Adults should see this not as a sign of disrespect, but rather as a cry for attention. I can already hear some of you saying, "Right! But how does one give adolescents positive attention when they are so rude and annoying?"

It's not as hard as it may seem. First, recognize that you are the adult in the situation. Look for ways in which you can provide positive attention, perhaps through something as simple as a smile. More time-consuming reinforcers include attending sports or other extra-curricular activities even if the adolescent in whom you have an interest is not directly involved, spending alone time with the youth, or doing special activities together such as going out for lunch. The following story concludes this section.

Angie had lived in various group homes all of her life. At the age of sixteen, she was to be placed with foster parents. Angie, who was not a particularly happy adolescent (likely for good reason) was anxious about the move. I worried silently for both Angie and her new foster parents. On the first morning of her new placement, Angie arrived at school carrying an innocuous brown paper bag. When I asked her how she was, she exploded with excitement. "They made me lunch. No one has ever made me lunch!" she cried happily. Angie carried her lunch with her all morning, and she never stopped smiling. Such a simple thing. . . the time and attention taken to provide a girl with lunch.

Rules

"Laws too gentle are seldom obeyed; too severe, seldom executed."

Benjamin Franklin

When asked what they found difficult about being an adolescent, two of the five most common answers were too many rules at school and too many rules at home. Adolescents accept the fact that they need rules, but cringe when rules control everything they do.

Life, unfortunately, does not work without rules. Here we have a huge conflict: many adults see rules as something to be made while just as many adolescents see rules as something to be broken. A point that needs to be stressed is that most adolescents do not break rules because they are bad, but because they want to be accepted by their peers. Nothing, and I mean nothing, will stand between an adolescent and his or her peers. Nevertheless, there must be rules. To begin, rules should be:

- specific,
- brief,
- limited in number,
- acceptable to both parties; flexible,
- inflexibly enforced and reinforced.

The following are two examples.

1. Never be late.

2. Be polite and courteous.

These rules are brief, but obeying or enforcing them will surely lead to arguments or differences of opinion. The first one – being on time – is a major concern with adolescents. It is important to create a rule about curfews or lates that states the expected arrival time and the consequence for tardiness. Creating a rule that simply requires the adolescent to be "on time" is too vague and will invite arguments. The topic of curfews is a private matter in each household. The one suggestion I would make, however, is that the time be decided on with the adolescent. Naturally, they will argue that "All the other kids get to. . ." or at school, "You are the only teacher who. . . ." Don't get angry! Think of the humor of this scenario. At the same time you are being assured of "other kids' curfews" or "other teachers who. . ." you are being used as an example by another adolescent. A good comeback is, "I understand, and I want to be fair. The reason I have set your curfew at _____ is _____. When you have proven that you can handle this time, we will discuss a possible change." This response is flexible in that it leaves the future of the curfew up to the adolescent, yet it is structured in that you have stated a time and a reason for this time. In addition, you have shown trust (and respect) of the adolescent by saying "when you have proven. . ." instead of "if you can prove. . . ." This slight difference in wording may seem frivolous, but adolescents will pick up on it immediately. Finally the brief rule might be: "You will be home by 10:00 weeknights and 12:00 weekends."

The issue of curfews is not unlike the "lates" issue with which teachers must deal, and the same principles apply. Obviously, the problem presented by the student who is frequently late for morning or afternoon arrival should be dealt with through meetings with the adolescent, his or her parent(s), and school personnel. A larger concern to teachers of adolescents, however, is the student who is perpetually late for classes. This issue always brings to mind Kitty, an intelligent girl who was late for every class, not through intent but through distraction. I had tried a number of flexible strategies to curb her lateness, but nothing worked. I then scheduled a conference with Kitty to discuss the problem, and to ensure that we understood each other's point of view. We brainstormed for ideas and selected one that seemed plausible, which was to attach a sticker to her hand each day as a reminder to be on time. For the next few days, I sought Kitty out as early as possible in order to give her the sticker and remind her of our arrangement. The next step was to meet her at the door of my class and provide positive reinforcement for being on time. This structure continued for five days. Thankfully, it was a successful ploy and Kitty, for the most part, is now on time for class.

Of course, this is just one occasion. Often there appears to be nothing that will encourage tardy adolescents to reform. There is no cure-all for this situation, but one method that appears to be slightly more effective than others is to lock your classroom door after a reasonable period of time (five minutes is appropriate), and begin your lesson. When the latecomer realizes the door is locked, it is his or her responsibility to knock once and then remain quietly in the hall until you are ready to open the door. Making the adolescent wait too long defeats the purpose and encourages him or her to leave. Once you become aware of the latecomer's presence, wait for approximately five minutes. When she or he is allowed in, enter the amount of time outside – the adolescent will have to make up this time after school. It is important that this scenario be discussed and understood beforehand, so that at the time of the tardiness, no reinforcement is given to the adolescent.

There will be some students who will be late deliberately so they can remain in the hall with peers; others may want to serve a detention and thus receive individual attention from the teacher; a few may enjoy the "look at me" aspect of walking in late. In any of these instances, the teacher must look carefully at the behaviors, try to discern the underlying reason(s) for them, and deal with both the cause and result.

Suggestions for home and school are interchangeable because adolescent-adult conflict over time is the same. In every case, the adolescent is dealing with the here and now while the adult is looking ahead. Thus it is necessary that we remain flexible (open-minded) at the same time that we maintain structure (consistency).

Too many rules make for the following of none. You know that when faced with a long list of regulations, you are more likely to dismiss all of them. A short, specific list that draws attention to the most important items will prove more effective. In both home and school settings, specific rules will differ but the general themes will probably remain constant. Appropriate areas for rules are issues of time, responsibility, personal hygiene, and safety. An example of a list of rules that keep within the limited number restriction, plus fill the above requirements, might be:

RULES FOR THE CLASSROOM

1. Be in the room and seated within five minutes of the bell.
2. Complete all homework.
3. Remain quiet and in your desk, even if you decide not to work.
4. Be considerate of others (e.g., feet under own desk, good grooming habits).

RULES FOR HOME

1. Pay attention to and uphold curfew.
2. Complete homework before a set time.
3. Follow a schedule of responsibilities around the house.
4. Call! Always let me (us) know where you are.

THREATENING RULES

Rules do not work if they are posed as threats. Consider the following:

- If you don't do _____, you'll lose your allowance.
- If you are caught chewing gum, you'll have to wash the hall floor.
- You'll have to scrub all the desks if you write on one desk.
- If you are late, you'll be grounded for the rest of the month.

Although the consequences might well be realistic, the threatening wording will surely cause rebellion on the part of the adolescent. These rules convey no trust; rather they assume that the adolescent will break the rule. They suggest structure, but in a negative manner. Consider the following rewording of the same rules.

- It is your responsibility to _____.
- Gum chewing is not allowed because of the damage gum does to the halls.
- Writing on desks is prohibited. This is vandalism of public property.
- Your expected time of arrival is _____, because _____.

True, the wording no longer contains the consequences of breaking the rules. Instead it contains an aspect of respect and faith in the adolescent, as well as at least a limited reason for the regulation. Again structure is stressed, but it is now more positive and flexible. Naturally, consequences will be discussed with the adolescents when the rules are established and implemented. Remember that when you assume the responsibility of rule making and enforcing, you are a dealer in hope, not revenge.

In summary, the saying "less is better" is applicable. Rules, like everything else in life, are subject to change (flexibility). Lift rules that are no longer necessary. Keep in mind that rules are made to provide adolescents with structure and assist them in the development of their own values. When asked what kind of discipline worked best, the majority of the adolescents responded, "Rules, as long as they are fair!" Rules provide an avenue of accountability and are not meant to control young people. They should be structured yet flexible enough to allow for human error and individualization.

Goals

When adolescents were questioned about what they saw in their future, far too many answered, "Nothing." The most common rationale for this response was not, as I had expected, society's shortcomings. Instead, they did not know how to set realistic goals and had already experienced considerable failure. Most had once had lofty ambitions (e.g., to be a pilot, a doctor), but believed these ambitions were not attainable because of a lack of employment in the area or their own limited post-secondary schooling. Although there is truth in what many believe, we can help these adolescents by being positive, and encouraging them to form goals that are attainable in the short term. Noble long-term goals have their place, but when the adolescent can't see past today, she or he needs to achieve goals in a relatively short amount of time.

In many instances, there are two issues at stake – the adolescent's goals and our goals for the adolescent. I will deal with the former first. Goal setting is a difficult subject for anyone, but as I have mentioned, it is especially so for the adolescent with his or her high ideals, coupled with a "live for today" attitude. Generally, impractical self-expectations lead only to failure. Thus, the first step is to convince the adolescent of the usefulness of goal setting for both major and minor achievements. I have found the following points to be useful in discussions regarding goal setting.

WHY SET GOALS?

1. They give us a focus; we know where we are headed.
2. They allow for self-evaluation.
3. They help us to recognize our own accomplishments.

Initially, many adolescents will set goals simply to satisfy the concerned adult(s), and this is fine. The act of thinking through and setting down in writing expectations for one's self is a worthwhile exercise. Chances are that the adolescent may well head toward his or her goals unconsciously. Once the adolescent has been convinced of the value of this action, we must guide the way. The following framework has worked for me.

1. Goals must be realistic. To ask a student who has been failing to try to achieve honors is a waste of time. A realistic goal would be to ask the student to increase his or her marks ten percent in all subjects. Similarly, to expect an adolescent who is always late to be punctual is setting him or her up for failure. Suggest a seventy-five percent improvement – the adolescent can be late once for every two occasions she or he has been on time. Increase the goal until the adolescent is punctual.

2. Goals must be specific. Saying, "Improve your attitude" is less effective than saying, "There will be no more frowning and complaining at the table!" Happiness is found more easily when goals are clear.

3. Goals must have timelines. Adolescents seldom think past tomorrow, let alone a month from now, so the shorter the time limit for the goal, the better. As an example, "Science marks will improve to seventy percent by the end of the year" is less effective than, "On the next science test, your mark will be above _____."

4. Goals should be reviewed frequently. It is pointless to set a realistic goal with an adolescent, and then not follow through with monitoring. We must discuss the goal on a regular basis, and assist the adolescent in evaluating his or her progress.

5. Goals need reinforcing. When goals are met, the adolescent must receive positive reinforcement immediately. Waiting until the end of the month is too long to be meaningful to an adolescent. If goals are not met in the allotted time, reinforcement is needed for any effort that has been made, and the goals need to be rethought. Alter the goal if necessary.

Remember that we all have goals and reinforcement built into our lives, the paycheque being one example. The smile on the face of a peer or spouse is another positive reinforcement. Adolescents need to be taught how to set goals for themselves, especially when the goal involves a less than pleasant activity for the adolescent. Let's face it, most adolescents do not want to keep their room tidy. It is we who desire this! So, it is our responsibility to help establish this goal appropriately and to reinforce achievement.

We know that the most important part of achieving is knowing what you want, yet frequently most of us don't know what we want for, or from, adolescents. Consequently, we have expectations that can only lead to frustration and resentment for ourselves and adolescents. We need to identify our expectations and examine the probability of the adolescent reaching them. For instance, expecting an adolescent to survive high school and never step out of line, no matter how "good" she or he has been until then is impossible! Similarly, expecting an adolescent to refrain from experimenting with smoking and alcohol is equally unrealistic. Think back – you experimented, didn't you? And yet you managed to survive. Have faith in the adolescent, and respect his or her ability to handle growing up. Be flexible in your reactions and your expectations; be inflexible in your support. And when the adolescent fails to meet your expectations (failure is a part of the maturity process), relax. You will both survive! Tomorrow is another day, a fresh new start, and a second (or third, or fourth) chance.

"The trouble with not having a goal is that you can spend your life running up and down the field and never scoring."

Dian Ritter

Space

Nothing does as much to tranquilize the restless or anxious mind as that of having one's own space. This often overlooked preventative measure – the provision of personal space – can help to avoid at least some of the difficulties experienced by adolescents and their families. When asked what age they would like to be, the most common response adolescents gave was to be old enough to have their "own place." There is a message there for us, and it is not simply that we must provide our youth with a bed and a closet.

The most natural and important space is the adolescent's bedroom, however not all will have their own room or bed. If this is the situation, a certain inventiveness is required. If the youth is lucky enough to have a room of his or her own, the adult must accept the adolescent's right to go there, lock the door, and be alone. In addition, it is the wise parent who allows the adolescent freedom to decorate the space as she or he sees fit. Keep in mind that an adolescent's taste tends to differ greatly from that of an adult, and it's only a room. The adolescent will be grateful for a room alone, but will only feel it is his or hers if given free rein in decorating. Limitations should encompass only unhygienic conditions or structural changes. The perpetual pile of clothes on the floor will not diminish with nagging, so why bother? For adolescents who must share a room, there is still the possibility of personal space. Half of the room, for example, could be his or hers with the same "do your own thing" approach. For the adolescent who must share a bed, there is a solution in that some part of a wall can "belong" to him or her.

At school, lockers and desks should be considered personal space. While I recognize that there is sometimes a need to open lockers, it can be considered a violation of privacy, as well as a show of disrespect. If lockers must be opened, it should only be as a last resort and with fair warning to the adolescent.

Why so much concern with private space? Think about it. We have desks, special corners, vehicles, or places that give us necessary aloneness. As well, most of us have places to display mementos, photos, and so on. Adolescents, although they crave these same rights, have very little they can call their own. Let's give them space!

Reinforcement

"All I ever hear is the bad stuff I do. I wish someone would sometimes mention the good stuff!" Although these are the words of an adolescent, most adults have experienced similar thoughts. When confronted with this issue, adolescents assure me that they never get enough "positives" and that even the tiniest pluses are worthwhile. When asked to be specific, they offered a variety of suggestions, the bulk of which make up this section on reinforcement.

The rationale for dealing with reinforcement in this chapter is that reinforcing the appropriate will often prevent the inappropriate. I'm sure that we are all tired of hearing about reinforcement, especially in relation to adolescents whom we don't see as deserving. This, then, is the first and foremost point. It is our responsibility to be alert to actions worthy of positive reinforcement.

I am guilty of allowing myself to be caught in the "she (he) -never-does-anything-to-compliment" syndrome. When writing report cards, it is generally the policy to share positive behaviors with the adolescents and adults who will be reading them. Struggling with the report of a young man, Ted, I blurted out, "How can I possibly say anything nice about Ted? He's the worst kid I have ever known – he'll never amount to anything!" Ouch! What a terrible thing to say. What right did I have to not only insult another human being, but also to suggest negative implications for his future. True, Ted was difficult. He always knew which buttons to push to annoy me. He never did his homework. He never studied. He was frequently rude, demanding, lazy, and uncooperative. Do you recognize this chap? Instead of dwelling on these behaviors that upset adults (he was a hit with his peers), I, as a responsible adult, should have focused on his strengths. Ted pushed my anger buttons because he was bright enough to know what they were. He never did homework or studied, yet he passed most tests. He was rude and demanding, but I had allowed that. As far as being lazy and unco-operative, I recalled the time when I asked Ted to help me with changing a tire, and he was wonderful. Perhaps I was seeing Ted only through tunnel vision.

HOW TO REINFORCE

Once the reason for reinforcement has been established, you must determine "how." The impact of social reinforcement – a hug, pat, wink, kind word, and smile – cannot be overlooked but there is more! Experience has taught me that a brief written note of reinforcement or appreciation works wonders.

One day, sixteen-year-old Shelly arrived at school with an unusually large smile and a bounce to her walk. She showed me a note that her foster mom had put in her lunch bag telling her what a great job she had done with the laundry the previous day. What a positive reinforcement it was for her.

One way to capitalize on this idea is to purchase inexpensive packages of blank cards on which you can write a few words of praise. Adolescents appreciate such notes. Naturally, the giving of small gifts or trinkets is always a successful positive reinforcement. The problem lies in purchasing items that the adolescent will like without your spending too much money in the process. After considerable trial and error, conversations with adolescents, parents and peers, and many hours spent wandering around malls, I have put together the following list of gift suggestions. One caution: the manner of giving is worth more than the gift. Try to accompany gift giving with a positive manner and words of appreciation or praise.

TYPES OF REINFORCERS

Reinforcers fall into so many categories that a thorough examination would be impossible. Instead, I have listed reinforcers (with the eager assistance of adolescents) according to cost.

Free Gifts
- hugs,
- your time (amount can be dependent on situation, should be flexible).

Gifts Under $1.00
- trinkets,
- unusual pencils, erasers,
- iridescent felt marker,
- small note pads,
- cards (e.g., baseball, fantasy),
- edibles.

Gifts Under $5.00
- playing cards,
- address books,
- felt markers,
- puzzle or maze books,
- comics,

- joke books,
- inexpensive jewellery (many adolescents, including boys, like chains, wristlets, pins),
- trinket boxes,
- coupons for fast-food restaurants,
- variety of "adult-type" items (e.g., key rings),
- items from a magic store,
- blank tapes,
- single rose (for male or female),
- magazines.

Under $10.00
- movie passes,
- meal vouchers,
- gift certificates from music, poster, and book stores,
- tapes (only if you are sure of the adolescent's tastes).

Over $10.00
- clothing,*
- hats,
- posters,
- gift certificates from a sports store,
- entrance fees for activities (e.g., a recreation centre),
- short-term memberships in health clubs (for older adolescents),
- ticket(s) to special events (e.g., sports, ballet, theatre),
- any type of stereo equipment,
- wristwatch (styles in these change regularly),
- identification bracelet,
- "beeper" and a month of time (additional time can be earned),
- magazine subscription.

* Here is a cautionary tale about buying clothing for an adolescent. On her sixteenth birthday, Meg's mother gave her a beautiful, expensive blouse. Her aunt gave her a black leather mini-skirt with silver zippers and buckles. Guess which item was put in the back of the closet for "sometime" and which was worn daily? Adolescents wear only what they want to wear, and nothing we do will change this fact! Purchasing something that only we like is unrealistic and disrespectful to the adolescent's taste.

You've probably noticed that no mention has been made of the gift of money. This is, and probably always will be, a popular gift. The problem with money as a reinforcement, however, is that it doesn't involve much thought on the part of the giver nor does it allow for individualization. Adolescents pay attention to, and appreciate, the time spent on selecting something for them. They want to be recognized as an individual – the giving of a dollar to all minimizes the power of reinforcement. While there are merits of "Here's $5.00 for cutting the grass," there are better reinforcers.

A final word on reinforcers – it is possible to give too much. Adolescents are aware of what they deserve and see bribery (over-giving of gifts) as wrong. Indebtedness to the giver will not make the adolescent grateful. There are times when positive reinforcement is inappropriate, and may be given to ease the guilt of the adult. Be wary of this trap.

"Among the smaller duties of life I hardly know any one more important than that of not praising where praise is not due."

Sydney Smith

CHAPTER FIVE

Discipline

"Adolescents today contradict their parents and tyrannize their teachers."

Socrates (470-399 BC)

If we were to believe the media depiction of adolescents – aimless, jobless, militant, delinquent – we would be tempted to think that this generation of adolescents far outranks its predecessors in terms of negative behavior. As this quote confirms, adolescents have long been considered somewhat of a thorn in the side of adults.

Given that today's adolescents are similar to those of earlier generations and that all civilizations comprise adolescent populations that have matured, perhaps we are making more of an issue of adolescence than is necessary. Adolescents *are* difficult, moody, and unpredictable. We were once the same. In fact, many of us are still difficult, moody, and unpredictable. For some reason, this is acceptable to society and allowances are made for difficult traits exhibited by adults.

That said, there are some serious and frightening situations involving adolescent violence, drug abuse, and vandalism. It is not my intent to make light of these – they will be dealt with later in this chapter. Rather, I would like to awaken in adults a renewed hope for our youth. If we can establish and enforce rules and expectations in a flexible yet structured manner, today's adolescents will stand a better chance of becoming tomorrow's successful adults.

When adolescents were asked what forms of discipline they had experienced and their effectiveness in curbing negative behavior, many gave fairly detailed answers, leading me to believe that they view discipline as an important issue. I was able to categorize their responses into two groups – successful and unsuccessful disciplinary tactics. This information, coupled with their views of what they suggest for specific misdemeanors, provided the basis for this chapter. It is interesting to note that many adolescents tend to be hard on themselves, and frequently suggest disciplinary actions that most adults would consider punitive and unnecessary.

How do we supply adolescents with the discipline they need and which they view as important? What are our duties when faced with inappropriate adolescent behavior? Where do we start? How do we handle serious difficulties? One way to begin is by differentiating between minor and serious misconduct.

Minor Misconduct

When an adolescent is out of line, begin by establishing the severity of the behavior. Silly mistakes should be viewed with humor, not discipline. We all make stupid mistakes. . . locking our keys in the car, searching for the glasses on our head, or dialing the phone only to forget who we are calling are adult examples of such mistakes.

Like adults, adolescents also make silly mistakes. They forget, lose or neglect items, and they can irritate us with their apparent lack of concern. It is important to remember that these are not serious crimes, and our responses should mimic this fact. In any event, no amount of punishment, counselling, or pleading will change these adolescent habits. It makes more sense, then, to find a way to reverse the actions of the adolescent at least some of the time. As an example, you can encourage the use of lists, task books, and reminders. These actions should be, to some degree, successful.

This is being flexible, and it can be scary. It can be helpful to remember that forgetfulness and disorganization are a normal part of maturation (at least in some cases). One day, the adolescent may surprise you with a 180 degree turn in behavior.

Serious Misconduct

There will be times when the need for discipline is absolute. Although we have varying levels of tolerance, the following behaviors are typically seen as punishable:

- theft (from home, peers, school, community),
- anti-social behavior (e.g., continual disrespect, sarcasm),
- constant violation of established rules (e.g., lates, curfews),
- brutality to others, including animals (threat or actual physical abuse),
- drug and/or alcohol abuse,
- vandalism (all forms),
- lying on a regular basis.

In dealing with any one of these misbehaviors, there are four major elements to be considered: anger, rescuing, accountability, and discipline.

Anger

Anger is a normal and healthy emotion, but when misplaced or demonstrated in a non-beneficial manner can result in counter-productive outcomes. If you recall, adolescents stated that the most irritating behavior of adults was yelling. If an angry person begins to yell, his or her target often has little choice but to yell back or completely block the flow of anger.

Neither of these responses will lead to a satisfactory conclusion. I am not suggesting that you, as the adult, ignore your anger but rather to channel it in a more flexible manner. The following suggestions have proven valuable to me over the years.

Time Out

The first step is to allow yourself a time out. Horace, "Epistles," referred to anger as "a brief madness." If this is the case, logical thought is impossible when one is angry so the forming of a fair judgment or decision is improbable. Scarlet O'Hara had the right idea when she said, "I can't deal with this today. I'll deal with it tomorrow." Obviously, Scarlet required a longer time-out than is seen to be desirable today, but the point is the same. Sometimes it is necessary to pull away in order to tackle a problem efficiently.

Arguments

> "Anger is never without an argument, but seldom with a good one."
>
> George Savile

You've likely found that it is virtually impossible to argue with an adolescent. They have an unending supply of excuses, comebacks, and not-so-nice words. Instead of allowing yourself to be caught up in a never-ending argument, take a few moments to explain calmly why you are angry. Use "I" terms and be specific: "I get angry when you turn away when I'm speaking to you" is better than "You make me mad when you're disrespectful!"

Typically, the first reaction of the adolescent will be denial. If this is the case, refuse to discuss the situation further at that time. Tell the adolescent that in the future you plan to ignore him or her if the same situation reoccurs. Follow through. The next time a similar scenario occurs, point out that this is "one of those times" in which she or he previously used denial. Look directly at the adolescent then turn away without discussion. The adolescent will get the message and the behavior will eventually lessen. Naturally, you will want to deal with the behavior later. The point is that you will have not given negative attention and the time and effort that this entails.

Arguing is an energy-draining action that serves only to escalate the powerful feelings already in control. How often do we say things we don't mean in the heat of an argument? We can later excuse these words with no damage to our ego; an adolescent does not have the experience to do this and can be crushed by a careless word. An argument leaves no room for solutions so it is up to you to be inflexible in stopping this downward spiral. The use of a phrase such as, "I refuse to argue about this. I'll discuss it with you later (e.g., in ten minutes, after school)" will expedite this.

Ignorance

Another point to consider is that ignorance can intensify anger. By this I am referring to situations where there is no obvious solution to a problem, no answer to a question, or no room for compromise. An argument about an adolescent's hair, for instance, often results in such a situation. Feelings of worth and pride interfere with logical thought, and each party will probably remain ignorant of the other's point of view. In a no-win situation such as this, the powerful adult thing to do is to be flexible and back down.

> "The most savage controversies are those about matters as to which there is no good evidence either way."
>
> *Bertrand Russell*

Extenuating Circumstances

Try to avoid conflict situations when you are ill, tired, or stressed. (For many of us, this is the case a great deal of the time.) It is important to remember that when burdened with one of these extenuating factors, it is easier to lose your perspective – an argument may end up in a power struggle. This is the last thing that both parties need. If you have an option, tackle the problem when you are feeling better. As an example, dealing with a child's falling grades is an issue you can put off until your migraine clears. The discussion will not have suffered because of the delay.

The same holds true for the adolescent. If she or he is tired or ill, this is not the time for a heart-to-heart talk. True, the adolescent may appear to be listening more co-operatively than usual, but your words will have little impact other than to possibly increase his or her fatigue.

The Power Struggle

Another no-win situation is the power struggle. Typically, adolescents believe their self-esteem is on the line in these situations, making retreat an impossibility. Similarly, the adult may believe that she or he cannot back down without losing face. The end result of these standoffs is often out-of-control anger on the part of both the adolescent and the adult.

A power struggle can erupt quickly when it centres on an issue that arouses strong feelings. The one difference between the adolescent and the adult in this situation is that the adolescent cannot control powerful emotions while the adult can. Therefore it is up to you, as the adult, to recognize topics that, when discussed, can become the focus of a power struggle. Here are a few signs that indicate that a discussion is escalating to a power struggle:

- raised voices,
- failure to listen,
- repetition of thoughts and words,
- heightened emotions,
- physical proximity,
- angry body language.

How can you de-escalate the issue?

- stop talking,
- move away but maintain eye contact,
- say, or indicate in some manner, "Stop!"
- touch the adolescent (only if it is necessary to temporarily restrain him or her),
- indicate calmly that the discussion will resume at a later time when both parties have had time to cool down. If the level of anger has become too powerful to allow this, remove yourself from the situation. Walk away, and return to the issue later.

What if the adolescent strikes out?

- do not hit back,
- try to speak calmly, protect yourself, and give the adolescent some physical distance. Try to remain with the adolescent until his or her anger cools then arrange for a discussion at another time.

Rescuing

The normal reaction of most adults is to want to rescue adolescents in trouble. By this I mean to step in, take the blame, accept responsibility, give in, or offer an "easy way out." Whatever the motive, rescuing is done from the heart rather than from the head, and in the long run hurts more than it helps. An examination of this seemingly altruistic action may help you to see it differently.

Jay was a quiet seventeen-year-old boy whose father was a single parent raising three children. As the oldest child, Jay had considerable responsibility in the home. This was his excuse for never doing homework or, in truth, anything at school. Jay's teacher invited the father and Jay to the school to discuss the situation. His father pronounced that Jay was a "good boy" and not at fault. The fault, he said, was with the school system. He would not allow his son to remain after school for additional help nor would he discuss the idea of a homework log. During the discussion, Jay sat with his head down and a small smile on his face. Jay had been rescued. He did not have to adjust his inappropriate behavior in any way.

Why did this happen? There is always the possibility of self-deceit on the part of the adult. Too often, what we wish we believe to be true, and it may be difficult to face reality. When confronted by someone whose opinion differs, the adult rescues the adolescent from him or her.

Some adults have been indoctrinated by "pop" psychologists to be tolerant and all-accepting of adolescent behaviors. The danger in this is that too much tolerance causes tunnel vision. The adult loses the capacity to differentiate between helping and hindering. Other adults express their infinite capacity for guilt through servile behavior. Although in all these cases the adult believes his or her actions to be in pursuit of adolescent respect, quite the opposite is true. Adolescents do not respect adults who are easily manipulated, and there is a fine line between helping and interfering.

The question, then, is how does one determine if an action is rescuing or assisting an adolescent? While this is a difficult issue that varies from individual to individual, asking yourself the following questions may be helpful.

1. Why am I coming to the aid of the adolescent?

2. Is the misbehavior silly or serious?

3. What will the natural consequences be if I do not involve myself in the situation?

4. Can the adolescent learn from these consequences?

5. Do I have respect for, and faith in, the adolescent?

6. Do I understand the situation, or have I been swayed by what the adolescent wants me to think?

7. Who am I helping – the adolescent or myself?

This final question poses yet another problem in the rescuing scenario, that of adult self-protection. As negative as this may seem, a lot of rescuing is done, possibly quite unconsciously, to protect the adult and not the adolescent. The adult cannot deal with the consequences of the youth's misbehavior and therefore denies it. Jay's father, for example, needed his son at home after school to look after younger siblings; he did not have time to assist Jay with his homework or to deal with a homework log. Innocent rationale, but the long-term effect to Jay could be devastating.

Parents are certainly not the only adults guilty of rescuing. I once intervened on behalf of Chris, a charismatic young man of fifteen. Although he never gave me any trouble, he was difficult with others. When he confided to me that he had been involved in theft from a corner store, I was shocked. He begged me to keep his secret, so when questioned I did not admit that I knew anything of the incident. Today Chris, a swarthy twenty-year-old, lives off the revenue from selling stolen goods. I didn't rescue him: I helped to condemn him. On hindsight, I question who the adult was in that incident.

How does one avoid this trap? First, assess the situation by answering the seven self-evaluation questions. If you think that you are being used, accept that you can leave the adolescent to deal with the problem on his or her own. Your lack of rescuing does not mean that your positive rapport with the adolescent is finished. Rescuing, like worrying, may seem like a viable way of showing you care, but adolescents may perceive it as a lack of confidence. In instances where you are tempted to rescue an adolescent, try using some of the following phrases:

- I can't do this because I would feel uncomfortable.
- I want to help, but this is not the way.
- I will support you, but it is your problem and you must deal with it.

These "I" statements indicate your acceptance of the adolescent and your unwillingness to play the rescue game. Adolescents know when and why they are being rescued, and will use a gullible adult repeatedly. Some become quite adept at manipulation, and do not hesitate to ply these skills to their advantage. Be aware that supporting these behaviors benefits no one. Instead, have faith in the adolescent's ability to deal with the consequences and support his or her efforts.

Think of rescuing as a reward for an unwanted behavior. Adult intervention reinforces inappropriate adolescent action. Is that what you want, or do you want the behavior to weaken or disappear?

Accountability

A colleague once said that the failure of society to cope with today's youth was a consequence of decreased accountability. After reflecting on his statement, I realized the weight it carried. Lack of accountability can lead to no action or inappropriate action. Have we lowered our standards so much that no one is accountable, including adolescents? As well, have we considered the band-aid solutions applied to problems arising out of this lack of accountability? The following story illustrates these points.

James was a lazy, charming grade nine student who had made little gain during the school year. When exam time came around, teachers provided James with peer tutoring, assistance, and study notes. The teachers wanted James to pass so they rescued him. Then, because James showed a bit of improvement, they decided to pass him to the next level, even though he didn't meet the requirements. The next year, James was enrolled in an altered program to compensate for his lack of knowledge. Thus James, through no effort of his own, was successful. Today James is a lazy twenty-year-old who lives on welfare and shows no desire to change his situation.

I do not mean to criticize teachers, parents, and professionals who do what they can to assist adolescents. Perhaps the issue is not intervention but expectations as a result of intervention. Given all the extra help he received, James remained unaccountable for his behavior. The question is, of course, how do we encourage accountability in people such as James?

Structure can play a large role in fostering accountability. The following suggestions, divided into two sections – school and home – suggest structure that, if maintained, encourages accountability.

- standardized tests.
- maintaining standards. If material is too difficult for students, break it into manageable segments, or skip some parts so that what is taught is understood.
- no continuous progress. Students must realize that they will not pass if they do not complete programs satisfactorily. The chance to repeat and try again is an important part of education. It is not punitive, and it is the adults' responsibility to support this premise.
- insist on academics. All areas of education are important, however, Mathematics, Science, and English must be treated as core subjects.
- consistent rule enforcement. There are several issues that make the enforcing of school rules difficult – too many rules, rules which are vague in wording, and staff inconsistency. Schools may find rule enforcement easier if staff agree on a few school-wide rules, then allow teachers to set their own "in-my-class" rules.

CAUTIONS FOR EDUCATORS

You will notice that no mention has been made of extra-curricular activities as a means of enforcing accountability. These should never be granted as a reward for academic achievement, or their removal as a punishment for poor marks or misbehavior. Perhaps it will help to realize that everyone is lacking in some area. Using a strength to create a sense of accountability for a weakness does not work. As with all suggestions, there are exceptions. The adolescent who has undertaken extra-curricular activities to the point where they interfere with his or her scholastic performance needs guidance. In this instance, it should be up to the adolescent (with adult support) to choose the activities she or he will continue.

After stating that standardized exams will increase accountability, I feel the need to remind educators of how traumatic exams can be for some students. Teachers can help with exam trauma by preparing students for exams (teacher accountability), and being supportive and flexible during the testing. As an example, refusing to allow a nervous student bathroom privileges during a two-hour exam is unnecessary and cruel. A better and obviously more flexible approach would be to arrange for the youth to be accompanied, if that is a concern. The flexible teacher who is enforcing the writing of an inflexible standardized test can remove some of the anxiety simply by being visible throughout the writing period, remaining alert to nonverbal cues of distress, and being ready to help.

In addition to the recording of standardized test results, I feel strongly that the wise educator should also assess the student against his or her own progress. When given together, these measurements provide a solid representation of the student's progress and abilities.

Accountability at Home

The basic premises for the promotion of accountability at school are also applicable to the home. Since the adult's goal is to assist the adolescent in becoming responsible, the first step is the creation of rules and responsibilities. There are other ways in which we can also help.

MAINTAINING STANDARDS

Once a standard (e.g., room cleaning involves changing sheets and vacuuming) has been set, it must be adhered to. Allowing slips on a regular basis can lead to eventual loss of standard.

SUPPORTING EDUCATION

Encourage accountability by insisting that your child complete his or her homework. As well, maintain regular contact with the school so that you are aware of and support educators' expectations of your child's schooling.

CONSISTENT RULE ENFORCEMENT

Rule enforcement at home often suffers from the same ills as rule enforcement at school. The most common home errors seem to be:

- too many rules,
- rules that are too vague,

- inconsistent rule enforcement, especially when more than one adult is involved.

ALLOWANCES

Adolescents should be allowed a regular allowance, the amount of which will depend on the situation. If the youth is to receive his or her allowance on Fridays, then the adult must be consistent in providing it on that day. There is nothing more frustrating to adolescents than to have to ask for what is theirs.

If extenuating circumstances make it impossible for the allowance to be given, the adolescent should be told about the circumstances honestly and promptly and alternate arrangements made.

It is my belief that allowances should not be taken away for punishment. Adolescents frequently expressed extreme dislike of this practice, and did not mention it as a viable means of discipline. In fact, many chose to add a line to the question regarding allowances indicating that withdrawing an allowance as a form of punishment was not effective.

EXTRA RESPONSIBILITIES

There are expectations of everyone in a family, and if these are to be prerequisites of an allowance, that is a private matter. However, I have come to the conclusion that it is better to leave the allowance as a separate entity, and provide payment for the completion of extra tasks.

As an example, raking leaves is a task that should not be expected to be done by the resident adolescent. Instead, a payment for completion of the job, according to preset standards, is appropriate. In addition, this makes the adolescent accountable – she or he must do the job properly in order to be paid. Just as we are accountable to our employers, adolescents are accountable for the jobs they complete.

KEEPING YOUR WORD

One of the most common complaints I have heard from adolescents is that parents ''aren't on time'' or ''aren't where they said they would be.'' This disturbs young people who have no control over the situation. Similarly, adults must say what they mean and mean what they say. Adolescents have an uncanny ability to remember what was said when the opposite was done. It's difficult to confront an adolescent who is armed with the words, "But you said. . . !"

CAUTIONS FOR PARENTS

The privilege of skiing, which is an important part of your life, is taken away from you because you were late for work several times. Would you consider this an infringement on your rights? In most instances, the answer would be "Yes." Like adults, adolescents need to see some correlation between their misbehavior and its consequence. What, for instance, is the correlation between "You can't go to your hockey game because you didn't do the dishes." I have found the use of "minutes of time" to be helpful on such occasions. One response to this dilemma could be, "It will take me thirty minutes to do your chore. You will lose that thirty minutes from your game. I'm sorry you can't play if you are late, but that is the consequence of your not doing the dishes."

Another situation where it is difficult to enforce adolescent accountability is one that involves the age-old, "because I'm older than you. . . ." This adult rationalization of lack of accountability frustrates adolescents. Better to admit to a weakness and the negative consequences of that behavior than to attempt to pass it off with this statement. This behavior gives adolescents lessons in avoiding responsibility – a quick adolescent will realize the universality of this excuse and adapt it for his or her own use. "I'm only a teenager. How was I supposed to know?"

Accountability is one component of responsibility and as such is difficult to isolate from other components. Although accountability increases with age, we should encourage it as a positive characteristic at all ages.

Discipline: Natural and Unnatural Consequences

"Whipping and abuse are like laudanum; you have to double the dose as the sensibilities decline."

Harriet B. Stowe

Despite our good intentions, there will always be times when the need for discipline is absolute. After considering the results of the questionnaire, I found that there was a general consensus on the part of adolescents concerning forms of discipline that do or do not work. I have divided these discipline types into categories of natural and unnatural consequences, although some may overlap.

Natural Consequences

A natural consequence is something that happens as a direct result of an action. For my purposes, this will be a reaction to an inappropriate action. Such a consequence, if it can be determined, is usually the most effective form of discipline. Sometimes, however, we overlook the evident and natural consequence in the heat of the moment. It is for this reason that I will review some of the most common adolescent misbehaviors and their natural consequences.

LOSS OF PROPERTY

It must be written somewhere that adolescents have to lose at least one item per day. If you have an adolescent at home, you no doubt find yourself empathetic to the turmoil she or he experiences as a result of losing or misplacing objects. To help your child with this problem, you can add structure through applying a natural consequence that encourages accountability. I doubt that the forgetfulness will disappear until adolescence is over (for some of us, it never disappears). For example, if your child loses an item, tell the child that she or he must replace the item or do without. If the item is a necessity (e.g., gloves in winter) and the child needs to borrow the money to pay for it, make arrangements where the child can work off the loan. Similar repayment plans can be carried out at school. One parent whose son lost a rather expensive jacket the first day he wore it realized he could not function in winter without a jacket. She took him to a second-hand clothing outlet where he had to purchase a replacement jacket. He was upset, but out of necessity he wore the jacket, and has lost no clothes since. If an adolescent loses something belonging to somebody else, replacement or repayment is his or her responsibility, even if this means borrowing and repaying the money.

BROKEN PROPERTY

If an adolescent breaks something such as a window, game, or watch, replacing or repairing the object applies since it is a natural consequence of the action. You break it; you pay for it. If money is unavailable, the adolescent may be able to arrange to repay with manual labor or time. One adolescent who broke a school window put in many hours assisting the custodial staff, at the reasonable rate of $10.00/hour, to make amends. Another adolescent who broke a tape deck at the home where she was baby-sitting paid for its repair with hours of baby-sitting.

IRRESPONSIBILITY

A single mother had assigned her son the task of doing the dishes nightly. Rick, aged fifteen, never seemed to have time to do them so his mother would do the dishes late at night. Then she imposed a natural consequence. She left the dishes until there wasn't a clean dish left in the house, and then she stopped preparing meals. After several days, the dishes were washed and the problem, for the most part, disappeared. A second example of irresponsibility involved a fourteen-year-old girl who refused to hang up her clothes. Her mother stopped doing her laundry. At first, this natural consequence did not seem to be effective, but eventually the girl begged her mother to wash her clothes. The mother assured the girl that she was capable of doing her own laundry, which she did. From then on, her clothes were kept in much better shape.

Both these examples link action with a natural reaction. In both instances, the adolescents were able to see how their irresponsible behavior affected others, and that it would not be tolerated.

DEFIANCE, RUDENESS, TESTING BEHAVIORS

It is difficult to determine natural consequences for these behaviors. Imagine how you would react if a peer behaved rudely to you. No doubt you would either fight or flee. Since neither of these approaches is appropriate when dealing with an adolescent, the best choice is to tell the adolescent you refuse to speak to him or her because of the behavior. This will block the behavior for the short-term – you can deal with the issue when both of you are more prepared to talk.

VANDALISM

The most obvious consequence is restoration of property by the adolescent responsible for the damage. If this is impossible, monetary retribution is necessary.

Automatic Natural Consequences

Sometimes natural consequences are instilled automatically. Such is the case with peer-enforced consequences. Peers, the most important persons in the life of an adolescent, have the ability to impose the most powerful consequences. For instance, consider the adolescent who is untrustworthy and reveals a secret with which she or he has been trusted. The natural consequence of this action is the negative reaction of other peers, especially when the "secret" is told to the person whose trust was betrayed. The result can be as severe as expulsion from the peer group. The potency of this natural consequence is obvious.

Peer pressure can sometimes be used by an adult. As an example, if an adult confronts the entire peer group and asks for input on consequences for a specific action, the adolescents will usually not only make suggestions, but help to enforce them as well. Here is an example of how peer pressure can be used by an adult.

Mark was a lazy adolescent, who, nonetheless, was charismatic and popular. His teacher was concerned with the number of students in the class who never finished their homework so he asked the students for assistance in changing the situation. They decided to create groups (of their own choosing), and delegated group leaders. The leaders then became responsible for seeing that members completed their homework. In order to be both flexible and structured, the students and the teacher decided that homework would be completed four-fifths of the time, thus allowing one miss per week. Mark, of course, was selected to be leader of the group comprising the worst offenders. The students also decided a reward, in this case ice-cream bars, would be given to any group meeting the criteria. (Eventually the students supplied the reward in the form of baking, treats, etc.) At the end of the first week, Mark's group was well behind the others, and fell considerably short of the target. The rest of the class commented on this, as did the members of Mark's group. In the weeks to come, Mark not only became a fair and authoritative leader, but he also assisted others in his group with their studies.

Unacceptable Natural Consequences

In some cases, the natural consequences of an action are not acceptable to the adult. Consider the "I have no pencil" school situation. The natural consequence would be that the student sits and does nothing, and is expected to complete the work later. Most teachers would rather supply the necessary materials than allow loss of instructional time.

The problem in this example is that the teacher supplies a solution rather than a natural consequence. A natural consequence might be the exchange of an item for the use of the pencil. The teacher can lend a pencil, but this generally means that it will disappear at the end of class. Through trial and error I have managed to come up with a plan that works for me. I purchase the ugliest pencils I can find. I lend these out, but since everyone knows these rather ugly pencils belong to me, students are more than happy to return them at the end of class. This is an example of preparing in advance for a situation which, from experience, has shown that natural consequences are not practical.

Unnatural Consequences

Disciplinary tactics or interventions are the structured results of an improper action, and are a necessary part of guiding adolescents. Although they cannot be classified as natural, they are, nonetheless, consequences of inappropriate behavior.

The questionnaire revealed many common disciplinary tactics, and there was a general consensus among respondents as to the degree of the effectiveness of each. The remainder of this section is a composite of the adolescents' responses.

GROUNDING

Adolescents seem to be divided in their evaluation of this widely used discipline. It appears that grounding works to a degree, but only under the following conditions.

- The adolescent is sixteen or younger. Older adolescents resent this treatment and view it as a "little kids'" punishment.
- The adolescent knows beforehand that a particular misconduct will result in grounding.

- The duration of the grounding is brief. By this I mean from a day to a week. Longer time frames only serve to make the adolescent angry and hostile. Some adolescents, faced with this scenario, decide to go out without their parents' knowledge, causing further difficulties.
- The adult who initiated the grounding must be visible to witness its enforcement. It is unfair to expect a fourteen-year-old to come home directly after school if she or he knows there is no one at home to witness the arrival.

LOSS OF TELEVISION OR PHONE PRIVILEGES

According to adolescents, this option works only for a short time since it is often forgotten or ignored. Adolescents suggest that adults consider the following points if they are going to take away these privileges.

- This option tends to work better with adolescents fourteen and younger. Older adolescents use a friend's phone or watch their television.
- The duration should be specified and reasonable. A week is usually as long as can be handled without supervision breaking down.
- Parents should suggest alternatives to watching television, for example, reading or completing homework.

LOSS OF AUTOMOBILE PRIVILEGES

This seems to be one of the best tactics to use with older adolescents. In fact, all that mentioned it felt that it made a bigger impact than any other form of discipline. The use of a car is a priority to an adolescent who will do almost anything to avoid the loss of this privilege. Similar "losses" would be the loss of the home for entertaining on a special occasion, or the loss of use of a school facility, such as the lunchroom.

DETENTIONS

Adolescents are almost unanimous in their declaration that this form of discipline does not work, having little or no effect on curbing misbehavior. That said, teachers are limited in what disciplinary measures they can employ, and detentions will always be a reality of the educational system.

The following suggestions, made by adolescents, may help make detentions somewhat more effective.

- The teacher must be in the place of the detention at the time of its commencement.
- When a detention is given, the teacher must not forget or cancel it.
- Detentions where students are expected to work are more acceptable to adolescents than those where they must sit until the required time has passed.
- Surprisingly, detentions, if handled in the correct manner (given and enforced calmly and consistently), are most effective with adolescents sixteen years and older.
- Adolescents who lack attention enjoy the one-on-one time detentions entail. Consequently, it is best to have minimum interaction between the adult and adolescent during the detention time. Acknowledge the adolescent's needs at a more appropriate time.

WRITING LINES

This appears to be a punitive, counterproductive action that angers adolescents and does little in the way of eliminating problem behaviors. If you use this as a form of discipline, have the students copy notes so that they have a chance to learn.

CORPORAL PUNISHMENT

An adult's angry outburst that involves corporal punishment does little to prevent further misconduct on the adolescent's part. Instead, such outbursts create fear, anger, and mistrust.

This type of discipline is often administered when anger has overtaken good judgment, or when an adult's fear for the future of the adolescent becomes overwhelming. It can be evidence of the adult's frustration and inability to cope with a seemingly indifferent youth. The adult may see the action as necessary, when in fact it is both counterproductive and cruel. (Fear is one of the main sources of cruelty.) Perhaps the adult sees in the adolescent his or her own weaknesses; perhaps the adult is replaying actions she or he experienced as a teenager; perhaps the adult knows of no other way to make a point. The reasons are valid – the action is not. In addition, other forms of discipline pale in comparison, necessitating ongoing and escalating corporal punishment.

We must accept the fact that when the impulse to inflict corporal punishment is strong, we have likely lost control and emotions override logic. If you find yourself in this situation, take time out immediately and deal with the behavior later.

> "No punishment has ever possessed enough power or deterrence to prevent the commission of crimes. On the contrary, whatever the punishment, once a specific crime has appeared for the first time, its reappearance is more likely than its initial emergence could ever have been."
>
> *Hanna Arendt*

YELLING

It is human nature to fling out loud, angry words when we are angry. According to adolescents, however, the thing they hate most about adults is that we yell. If we were to say the same words without yelling, would adolescents accept them? The unanimous answer seems to be "Yes" if adults do not:

- put the adolescent down,
- insult him or her,
- speak to the adolescent in front of peers,
- treat the adolescent as a child,
- make him or her feel guilty,
- refuse to let the adolescent speak.

MENTAL DISCIPLINE

This game, which some adults unfortunately like to play with adolescents, consists of abusing the character of the young person in some way. An example would be the statement, "You are so stupid!" While adults have the maturity and experience to put an insult in perspective adolescents are not so fortunate. Put downs are "pushaways" that serve no purpose other than to alienate the adolescent.

A more insidious type of mental discipline is the refusal to acknowledge the adolescent – the withdrawal of attention – because the adult is angry or frustrated. Sayings such as the following are a type of mental cruelty:

- I don't want to hear it.
- I'm not listening.
- I want nothing to do with you.
- I refuse to talk with you.

It is far better to use statements such as:

- I can't discuss this right now. I will talk with you later.
- I am too upset to speak at the moment.
- Please allow me some time alone before we discuss this issue.
- I am angry. I don't want to be near you in case I say something I will regret.

A third form of mental discipline is what I call the meaningful glare. To the adolescent who struggles daily with self-concept, this is as hurtful as a blow to the face. Looks of frustration, annoyance, and confusion are more easily handled by the adolescent. These expressions do not attack his or her sense of worth, but still convey the message that you are upset. We need to remember adolescents' sensitivity to non-verbal communication, and be aware of what we convey through our actions.

I have tried, as both a parent and teacher, to keep in mind that adolescents don't need reasons to do things as much as they need reasons not to do them. Therefore, we need to institute a structure of fair and consistent consequences for misbehaviors, but be flexible enough to consider circumstances in every situation.

The following pages contain some thoughts on serious crimes, such as theft and violence, the numbers of which seem to increase daily. Criminal actions, unlike other misbehaviors discussed in this book, involve more persons than significant adults. Some of us will be or have been involved with adolescents who commit these acts, and this involvement will never be pleasant. Surprisingly, most adolescents who completed the questionnaire believe tougher penalties should be imposed for young offenders. The following section reflects their opinions, together with the opinions of many concerned adults.

Adolescent Violence

The following misbehaviors are serious, often criminal acts that require grave adult reactions (there is no room for flexibility here; structure is the key):

- vandalism,
- theft,
- breaking and entering,
- cruelty to peers, adults, children, animals,
- attacking another, especially with a weapon,
- fear tactics (e.g., gang threats),
- drug/alcohol abuse.

Most of you will remember being involved in at least one of these actions during your own adolescence, but probably to a minor or limited degree. We know that adolescents are going to experiment with misbehaviors during these restless years, and not all of these misbehaviors should be considered indications of antisocial or criminal personalities.

As a society, however, we cannot deny our awareness of a small number of young people today who are committing terrible crimes. Several theories have attempted to answer the question of why adolescent crime seems to be increasing in both frequency and severity. One theory is that the media focuses on adolescent crime for its shock value. Consequently, there may only appear to be more adolescent violence than in the past. Another theory points out that with the drastic increase in the world's population, there are more adolescents with whom to deal. Yet another theory states that our society does not promote good behavior on the part of adolescents because the world that awaits them is in chaos – they are, quite literally, the scapegoats of society. A fourth theory proposes that if one is not involved in gainful and constructive activities one will become involved in destructive activities. Whatever theory we believe to be true, we need to be aware of the underlying reasons for adolescent crime and what we can do to stem this tide.

Possible Reasons for Adolescent Violence

1. Anger. Many adolescents must deal with physical and emotional deprivation. The consequence of this is anger aimed at a society that cannot protect them from such deprivations, now or in the future. We, as the adults and therefore the makers of this society, are the indirect targets. While there may be little that we can do to change some of these adolescents' opinions, we need to look at how we allow and

encourage the media's false depiction of success that sets up adolescents (and a great number of adults) for failure.

2. History. Unfortunately, some adolescents follow in the footsteps of significant adults who have a history of violent behavior.

3. Family. Breakup of the nuclear family seems to be more damaging to adolescents than we realize. This is a reality that all of us must face. Many adolescents desperately seek a place to belong. If they feel the family cannot offer them this security, they will seek it elsewhere and in the process may leave themselves more vulnerable to negative influences.

4. Too Much Time. Many young people lack the funds needed to participate in organized activities. As a result, they have little to do with their time, save meeting friends at malls, parks, arcades, and so on. A group of restless youths can easily be led by one who is more aggressive and angry than his or her peers. This may lead to crime since peer pressure will not allow for divergence from the leader and the rest of the group.

5. No Money. Given the scarcity of jobs, many adolescents have no money to call their own. As well, many families today find it difficult to finance anything more than the bare necessities of living thus making allowances impossible.

6. School. A number of adolescents point to the school system as being one of the major causes of teen violence. Instead of enjoyment and learning, school seems to represent a jail. The reasons and remedies for this would constitute another book.

7. Severe Personality Disorders. Sociopaths, or psychopaths depending on which term you prefer, often exhibit a lack of conscience at a young age – a predictor of future behavior. Because of their lack of emotion, they can be the most difficult group with which to work. Accomplished liars, such adolescents are charming, irresponsible people who, for the most part, don't respond to discipline.

Dealing with Adolescent Violence

Adults who have tried in vain to keep adolescents out of trouble must stop assuming the blame. Accepting the fact that there is nothing more that could have been done is a difficult truth for many of us to accept. This is the basis of tough love – when you know you have nothing left to give, you allow yourself to exit the situation or, at the very least, to refuse to support the behavior. If the adult continues to support, fight for, or rescue a lost youth, so too will the adult be lost. On these occasions, the law must intervene.

Adolescents who commit serious crimes must be dealt with in a humane but severe manner. Violent behavior on the part of the young should not be excused because of their age. If the punishment is to fit the crime, then incarceration may well be the only punishment. When asked what could be done about adolescent violence, the majority of respondents suggested harsher punishments such as longer jail sentences. As well, they suggested that community work was only a weak deterrent to adolescents and that adults were "wimps" for not taking a stronger stand on the issue of adolescent violence.

Older adolescents (sixteen and older) may be sent away from a family or school because of their incompatibility with society and its rules. This is not the end of the world for young offenders, and is a viable solution for some severe adolescent misconduct. Possibly the worst result of this scenario is the relentless guilt suffered by involved adult(s) who forget that in some situations it is best to pull away in order to gain perspective and deal with the problem. Once the decision has been made, only the adult will suffer guilt; the adolescent will suffer regret. And in the long run, perhaps that is the first step toward improvement. Every person has an obligation to fight for self-actualization – sometimes cutting ties and starting fresh is the only way to meet this obligation.

Finally, it is possible that the amount of attention adolescent violence receives from society is both reinforcement and stimulant. Why is it that we focus on criminal actions when positive adolescent contributions are barely noted? One small way neighborhoods, educational systems, and individual teachers and students can help to change this situation is through the creation of small newspapers that feature adolescents who are working for positive change. Perhaps local newspapers could include a regular column on adolescents that details their positive contributions to society.

Adolescent violence, while it is a fact that cannot be overlooked, is not indicative of all or even most adolescents. We need to remember that adults are also not immune to these behaviors, and that our struggling society influences more than adolescent misbehavior.

The nurturing of the young of any species requires adult affection, guidance, support, and discipline. The first three are the easiest; the fourth, discipline, encompasses these elements as well as thought and consistency.

"A true philanthropist, like a good parent, brings people to the point where they can help themselves. He offers them the gift of not being dependent on him."

Tao Te Ching

CHAPTER SIX

Topical Issues

"Life is the art of drawing sufficient conclusions from insufficient premises."

Samuel Butler

The last section of the questionnaire comprises twelve questions that focus on aspects of adolescent life that typically cause adults — parents and teachers — a great deal of concern. Respondents were asked to use these questions as discussion openers, or as topics for written compositions.

The content of this chapter, organized around these twelve questions, is intended to represent the thoughts adolescents had concerning these issues, as well as their opinions on what we, as adults, can do to help them cope. The material is presented somewhat differently from other chapters. For ease of reference, I have repeated the question as it appeared on the questionnaire. This is followed by a sample response from the questionnaire and general notes on the issue.

About Grades

Often people's marks tend to slip when they reach junior high. Has this happened to you? Why do you think this is a problem? Please suggest a way in which adults can help you prevent or overcome this problem.

Gary, aged thirteen:
"My marks have really dropped, and so have my friends' marks. I think it's because there are so many other things happening. In elementary, we just went to school. Now there's lots of sports, dances, going to the mall, and stuff like that. School just doesn't seem so important right now."

Chris, aged eighteen:

"In junior high, I was failing. I was too interested in fooling around. But now in grade twelve, I am working really hard and my marks are good. I guess I had to grow up a bit. No one could make me change. I just did it myself. But I can tell you one thing, the more adults bugged me in junior high about my marks, the less I wanted to improve them."

Based on responses to the questionnaire, the majority of adolescents recognized and accepted the fact that marks would or did fall during early adolescence. Those who were in their late adolescence typically reported that their marks improved as they got older.

Adults frequently worry when the scholastic achievement of a young adolescent drops. This is a natural phenomenon, due to rapid emotional and physical growth, hormone surges, and peer pressure, all of which take precedence over school work. Take comfort in the fact that most adolescents experience the same drop in marks – your underachieving "A" student who is now a "C" student will likely revert to his or her earlier level of achievement in a year or two. The following story illustrates a more extreme example of this phenomenon.

Karen was a perfect student and child. In elementary school, she was active in sports, music, and dance. Naturally, everyone expected that she would have a smooth transition to junior high. Not so. Even Karen was surprised to find that she no longer cared about school, and only attended so that she could spend time with her friends. Her marks dropped drastically and, as she put it, "Everyone was on my case!" Alarmed by this situation, Karen's parents and teachers hounded her about her lack of performance. Eventually, she dropped out of school and left home. Several years later, she returned to high school where she received honors standing. Karen, who is now a dentist, believes that the major focus of educational systems serving young adolescents should be the promotion of learning as interesting and as an end in itself. Attaching less importance to achievement will help students bridge the gap from elementary school to high school.

Try not to panic when you see a young adolescent's grades fall. Remain firm in your support of education, but don't overreact. Be structured and consistent in your faith in the adolescent (know *why* you trust him or her – there are probably many reasons) and be flexible in your expectations.

"What one knows is, in youth, of little moment: they know enough to learn."

Henry Adams

About Homework

How do you feel about homework? How can adults make this activity easier for you?

Cary, aged fifteen:
"I really hate homework because it interferes with my social life, but I guess I can see why it is necessary. What I hate most is when I have about three hours one night, and only a half-hour the next night. Teachers should work it out so that this doesn't happen. I hate it when my parents bug me and bug me to do it. Sometimes I just don't feel like doing it, and I know I'll get into trouble and I'm willing to accept that. I want to have some control over this myself."

The only variance reported in the questionnaire regarding homework was the degree to which adolescents disliked it. They admitted, however, that some homework was necessary.

Although I have cautioned against overreacting to a drop in grades on the part of young adolescents, I do not mean to imply that adults forget about or ignore the educational process. Above all, the adolescent must learn *how* to learn. Facts and figures will be forgotten, but the ability to learn, to study, and to absorb knowledge will be what leads the adolescent to success.

Homework, I realize, is a nightmare for parents and adolescents alike. Too often power struggles erupt, the homework may be only partially done, or not done at all. Given these problems, why do teachers continue to assign homework? The answer to this question is that homework is an excellent way of teaching students individual learning skills, as well as an effective means of reviewing materials taught in class.

We need to think of homework as the responsibility of the adolescent. What we can do to help is to set the structure for homework by making the inflexible point that homework will be done. Once this has been established, do not belabor the point. You cannot force an adolescent to absorb knowledge or practise skills if she or he is unwilling to do so. Here are suggestions that allow for both structure and flexibility, and that might help to encourage the adolescent to complete his or her homework.

1. Establish a specific place for homework completion, and encourage the adolescent to use this space each day. Such consistency encourages better work habits and provides some structure for the activity.

2. Together, establish a specific time for homework, and help the adolescent to start at this time. Keep the time free of other commitments such as family discussions. If necessary, remind the adolescent only one time about homework – if you mention it more than once, it will be perceived as nagging. As a general rule, a twelve-year-old should be able to do about one hour of homework in one night. This time period will gradually increase until the seventeen- or eighteen-year-old can complete as much as three or four hours of homework in one night. (These figures are not intended as an average, but rather what the adolescent is capable of in terms of his or her concentration span.) If the adolescent ignores this structure, implement a predetermined consequence.

3. Be interested. Ask the adolescent what she or he must do for tomorrow and be ready to assist if necessary. Do not hang over his or her shoulder or make constant checks to assure that the adolescent is on task. Remember that you cannot make the youth work. At best, you can facilitate homework by establishing some structure, then flexibility takes over and the adolescent must be left to his or her own devices.

4. Provide some sort of reinforcement for doing homework. Homework is not always fun nor is it intrinsically rewarding for most adolescents. Think about how you feel when you have to take files home from work and how this infringes on your private time. Adolescents experience these same feelings of infringement, perhaps with even more vengeance than those experienced by adults. If you can incorporate a "pay off" of some kind into the homework ritual, it will be helpful. This can be as simple as a few positive comments given on a daily basis, or a social activity that is earned after several nights of successful homework completion. Other actions that seem to work on a day-to-day or short-term basis are extended curfews and/or extra television time on a specific night. Keep

in mind that the negative does not work but the positive does – this is the flexible part of the homework scenario.

5. In some instances, homework sheets or books are available for students who have difficulty remembering the work for which they are responsible. Schools probably already have such sheets, but any adult can design one to fit an adolescent's needs. The following is intended as an example.

Day	Homework Assigned	Due	Teacher Initial on Completion

6. When faced with the "I have no homework" excuse, maintain the structure of the established time/place, but provide the adolescent with a book to read, a newspaper article to transcribe, or a letter to write. The idea is to maintain the routine at all costs. If you insist that the adolescent do something constructive and academic during the allotted time, eventually she or he will bring work home regularly. After all, if the adolescent has to work, she or he might as well do homework and thereby receive positive reinforcement from the teacher.

7. Homework is more than completing assignments. It is studying, reviewing, correcting errors, organizing notes, working on major assignments, and taking pride in work done well. Adolescents need to be reminded of this truism regularly. It is often effective to brainstorm (at school with a class; at home with a son or daughter) for all the things that can be considered homework. A chart posted in the homework area that lists these activities draws the adolescent's attention without involving you.

About Apathy

When people have little or no interest in the world around them and do not want to do anything to change their life, they are sometimes referred to as apathetic. As an example of apathy, some adolescents seem unmotivated and unwilling to put effort into school and/or home responsibilities. Do you fit this category? What do you think is the main problem affecting youth today?

Sandy, aged fourteen:
"I'm not apathetic. . . just lazy! It's not the same is it? All teenagers are like this. We just like to hang out. I'd work if I thought it would get me someplace, but it won't."

Apathy is, unfortunately, not limited to the adolescent segment of our population. It is equally common in the adult population. A search for the reasons behind this would probably result in a finger being pointed at our struggling society. However, this book deals with the "what now?" rather than the "why." There is no cure for apathy! It is a reality – a symptom of a shaky self-concept – a defense against failure, which, by its very nature, causes the failure in the first place. And adolescent apathy is one of the biggest difficulties facing teachers and parents today. What can we do? Since, as I pointed out, this is an evil with no remedy, the best we can do is to provide enough antidote to make the situation bearable. The following suggestions, which are both flexible and structured, may be helpful.

Look for the Niche

We must pay close attention to adolescents so that we can help them to uncover an area of interest or ability. Often an adolescent who is apathetic in class will eagerly give all his or her attention to another task. Charles is an example of this type of student.

In grade nine, Charles went into a slump. He refused to participate in academics, including subjects he had been known to enjoy. His manner remained civil, and his behavior continued to be relaxed. When queried, Charles would shrug and answer with a vague, "I don't know," or "I don't care." His behavior at home was the same, and no one seemed able to dent his armor of apathy.

Then came the school drama production. By chance, Charles was assigned the demanding job of Production Technician. It was as if a good fairy had tapped him on the shoulder, for suddenly Charles changed. He became the most eager, industrious, and capable technician the drama department had ever enjoyed. His skills became so great that every one was afraid to make a move without Charles's permission. Staff watched this transformation with amazement.

How did this happen? Obviously Charles found something at which he was good, and which offered immediate gratification. However, he continued to be apathetic toward his school work. Charles apparently hadn't yet learned the necessity of academics. In his mind, he would be able to be a first-rate technician without further schooling: he was a natural. At some point, Charles must have discovered the truth, and conscientiously acquired the missed education. Today he is completing his training as a Theatre Technician.

Perhaps this is the answer. Perhaps it is not that adolescents are apathetic, as Sandra suggested, but rather that they see no future in what they are doing and consequently experience no gratification. To circumvent this, we must be prepared to justify learning and suggest directions for adolescents to investigate, based on their interests and skills. We can also offer as much diversity as possible in educational programming, both at school and at home so that there is a greater chance of kindling a spark of interest. Suggestions to facilitate interest include field trips to the workplace, attendance at career conferences, guest speakers, and visits with parents to local businesses and institutions.

Reinforce the Insignificant

Of course, it is not possible to find that niche with all adolescents so we must try to reinforce even the smallest hints of motivation. When an adolescent accomplishes something worthwhile, no matter how small, it is worth reinforcing in a genuine manner. Although it may seem silly to reward such innocuous behaviors, sometimes that is the only place to begin. A good antidote to apathy is gratification.

Enforce the Physical

Sometimes a change of pace can interrupt a cycle of apathy. As an example, a brisk, structured, and enforced run (i.e., "This is not an option. You will all participate!") may be enough to shake the apathy, at least temporarily. It is a well-known fact that physical exercise increases the endorphins in the body, resulting in a sense of well being and/or elation.

There is no point in scolding, nagging, threatening, or attempting to coerce an adolescent out of his or her apathy. These are counterproductive actions at best. A brief discussion outlining your concern, in a relatively light-hearted manner, and offering a suggestion will suffice. If this doesn't work, remain calm and flexible. Becoming upset will cause a headache (for you), during which the adolescent's apathy will take on new and larger dimensions.

Not only is apathy disabling, it is also contagious. It is important for the adult to remain positive. Continue to be supportive, and do not dwell on the adolescent's apparent disinterest. Eventually something will happen that will cause the youth to become active, and then you can be ready with reinforcement.

About Independence

What concerns, if any, do you have about the amount of independence you have?

Angie, aged fourteen:
"Adults don't trust us. That's why they want to know every thought we have and every move we make. I think we should be allowed more freedom than we get. Then if we mess up, it can be taken away. Whatever happened to innocent until proven guilty?"

Most adolescents stated that they wanted more independence, but all agreed that they must first prove their ability to handle it. Adolescents aged sixteen and older felt that they required almost total independence in all areas of their lives, save self-support. The concept of being accountable only to themselves is obviously an appealing one for adolescents. Given their desire for independence, we can help them by encouraging independence in areas that are safe and follow an appropriate pacing. The following suggestions have worked in the classroom and can be adapted for the home.

- Allow adolescents to accept responsibility for their actions. Do not rescue them.
- Respect and trust adolescents.

- Provide them with an allowance that has "no strings attached."
- Provide for uninterrupted time alone.

Suggestions made in earlier pages foster adolescent independence. In fact, independence is what we should seek for the adolescent. A common complaint to this is, "How can we give them independence when they don't deserve it and can't handle it?" The truth is that although adolescents want independence, they are often not willing to exert effort to this end. This, again, is normal adolescent behavior, but is subject to maturation (thankfully). Witness the number of older adolescents who return to school to finish courses that they failed in earlier years or decided not to enroll in because of the level of difficulty involved. For the young adolescent, independence is limited, but begins with mutual respect. In addition to suggestions made previously, there are a few additional ways in which we can help.

FOR ADOLESCENTS AGED THIRTEEN TO FIFTEEN:

a. Younger adolescents should be allowed to have sleep-overs. We must be prepared to not only give permission to attend one of these gatherings, but also to host one or two at our home.
b. Parties are a must. Younger adolescents should have a chaperone who can try to remain invisible. Older adolescents must be trusted to attend unchaperoned parties.
c. Adolescents at this age are often flattered to be thought old enough to travel alone (within reason).
d. If possible, supplying the adolescent with a beeper provides not only more independence for him or her, but also a sense of security for the adult who can always contact the adolescent. I realize this is fashionable, but I have witnessed several instances where it was beneficial.
e. Allow adolescents to remain at home alone for longer periods of time.

FOR ADOLESCENTS FIFTEEN AND OLDER:

a. Allow the adolescent increasingly longer periods away from home without having to report in. The first time an adolescent goes camping with peers, for example, is a scary time for all, especially adults. This is where trust plays an important role.

b. Use of the family vehicle is a big step toward independence.
c. Use of the family home for unchaperoned parties is another example of faith in the adolescent, and gives him or her a feeling of growing independence. Remind the adolescent that she or he is responsible for the guests *and* cleaning up.

Obviously every situation is unique, and money is always a major factor. One thing, however, remains constant – independence is the first step toward success, and it begins with the faith of adults in adolescents.

> "Faith is to believe what you not yet see; reward for this faith is to see what you believe."
>
> *Saint Augustine*

About Peers

Explain the importance of the time you spend with other adolescents.

Kevin, aged fourteen:
"Well, they are the most important part of my life now. They never used to be. I'd always tell my dad things and he'd advise me. Now I tell my friends. My dad doesn't understand me anymore."

Everyone knows the importance of peers to an adolescent, but often the true intensity of these relationships amazes adults. There comes a time when even the most affectionate and devoted sons and daughters pull away from their parents. This is bound to cause alarm, confusion, and hurt on the part of the parents. In addition to peers, other people such as teachers, a friend's family, or other adults can also assume additional significance. The main thing for parents to do is remain calm, allow the adolescent to pull away, and try not to feel threatened. This "change of loyalty" is a normal progression toward adulthood. When the adolescent is eighteen or nineteen, she or he usually re-establishes family bonds. In the meantime, however, you can expect some, or even all, of the following behaviors from the young adolescent:

• secrecy – no more confident sharing of secrets and tales,
• sullenness when around parents; joy when around peers,
• phone calls, phone calls, phone calls,
• inability to make a decision without first conferring with peers,

- animosity directed toward once-appreciated family activities,
- open defiance, especially if the parent says something negative about a peer,
- overprotectiveness of peers, to the extent of jeopardizing self,
- reticence to respond to personal questions,
- increased moodiness.

Parents' options are limited during this time, save practising patience and flexibility. As Shakespeare said in "Hamlet," "Though this be madness, yet there is method in't." Realize that this apparent madness is a normal part of growing up, then go and read the paper. You would be wise to avoid the following:

- discriminating against peers,
- challenging the adolescent's secretive behavior,
- insisting on the continuance of established family activities that do not include peers,
- questioning the adolescent on a constant basis,
- refusing to allow the adolescent's friends in the home,
- reminiscing about times when the adolescent was younger,
- feeling guilty,
- insisting on behaviors that are known to be unacceptable to peers, such as wearing a particular item of clothing.

When Peers Are a Problem

For the most part, peers and the pressure they exude are more of an inconvenience to adults than a problem. There are times, however, when an adolescent will be misled by a peer group into what we know to be a dangerous situation. If you find yourself in this instance, check that what you believe is true – hearsay is not enough – then think through how you will handle the situation. Take a stand and be prepared for hostility on the part of the adolescent. The following structured plan illustrates how flexibility can be incorporated to make the situation easier for the adolescent to accept.

"I am concerned about what I see happening with you and your friends. Allow me to talk first, then you will have a chance. I know that your truancy and tardiness (at school) have increased drastically because the principal called me to discuss the problem. I know you were with your friends and while there is nothing wrong with that, I can't allow you to do this on school time. Even if you don't agree with me, I believe school is important. In fact, I'm so sure of this, I'm willing to make a deal with you. By the end of two weeks, you will have stopped skipping and will have reduced your lates by half. Then I will allow you to have your friends here for three hours each _____. I will stay in _____ and won't interfere with your time."

This hypothetical talk illustrates the basic tenets of adult intervention in a situation where peer relationships are a problem. Consider the following:

- peers are not rejected or put down,
- adolescent is not asked to leave the peer group,
- rationale is given for the decision,
- "I" statements are used,
- flexibility is shown by the lack of discipline,
- structure is shown by the expectation that the adolescent will co-operate; no other alternative is given nor will one be accepted,
- change is not expected immediately,
- reinforcement is built in.

I am not suggesting that you memorize a speech, but rather that you think through what it is you expect and why, and what you are willing to do to make this expectation a reality.

Putting Peers to Work for You

The old cliché, "if you can't lick'em, join'em," fits this idea. Given that an adolescent's peers are not going to disappear overnight, we need to turn their presence to our advantage. Here are some suggestions for what might seem an impossible task:

- Make friends with the peers, or at least do not make enemies of them.
- Ask the peers for suggestions for gifts, parties, and so on for the adolescent.
- Invite peers to accompany the adolescent on outings.
- Make use of peer tutoring in the classroom and at home. Sometimes an older adolescent can be of great assistance by tutoring a younger adolescent on a regular basis. The fact that the older adolescent is a peer to be looked up to is useful. I

witnessed the successful implementation of a school tutorial program where grade ten students were paired with grade eight students. Such a situation creates responsibility in the older student, and a sense of importance as well as a desire to please the tutor in the younger student.

- Give responsibility to one adolescent for the behavior of his or her peers. This works best when the responsible adolescent has some measure of control over his or her peers. Occasionally, the responsible adolescent may be the worst behaved, but improves greatly when given this new task.

There will always be adolescents that "run with the pack" and end up in trouble. At this time of their lives, many adolescents are drawn to danger, possibly because of the need to take risks, to feel the excitement of the illicit, and to turn their backs on everything for which society stands. While this is normal, it sometimes leads to undesirable behaviors enacted in the presence and for the benefit of the peer group. If this is the case, apply specific disciplinary actions. Older adolescents (seventeen to nineteen) are less likely to be influenced by peer pressure or to move in the large groups that younger adolescents favor. This demonstrates a growing maturity and self-confidence, and is wonderful to watch. The young man who, at thirteen, would not brush his hair without conferring with peers now sports an original hairstyle with pride. With the exception of gangs, who usually fall into the category of misbehaving adolescents and require serious interventions, most adolescents outgrow their need for peer groups and permission.

An adolescent's peers are his or her world for several years, so we must accept this and not come between them in all but the most dire instances. This is a developmental stage in forming friendships that we all must pass through in order to form strong, lasting friendships.

> "The communicating of a man's self to his friend works two contrary effects, for it redoubleth joys and cutteth griefs in half."
>
> *Francis Bacon*

About Dating

At what age do you think adolescents should be allowed to go on unescorted dates? What restrictions do you think should be placed on dating?

Chris, aged fourteen:
"I think this depends on the kids. What is really bad is when one of your friends gets to date and you don't. And I don't mind my mom picking me and my girlfriend up to take us home, but it's really gross if your mom hangs around."

Results of the questionnaire indicated a general consensus on the age when adolescents could begin dating. In general, most adolescents felt fourteen or fifteen was a good age to date, and that dating in groups was preferable to dating alone unless the adolescents were sixteen or older. There was also unanimous agreement on the part of younger adolescents (thirteen to fifteen) that parents not accompany their children on dates. They thought, however, that the availability of adults (e.g., as chauffeurs, in another part of the house) was important. Older adolescents (sixteen and older) expressed, quite naturally, the need for total independence on dates.

The junior high years are the time when dating often becomes an issue. There are no rules or guidelines concerning the "right" age to begin dating. Some precocious eleven- and twelve-year-olds will "go out" together as a couple for months while there are adolescents who are eighteen years old and have never had a date. We cannot predict when an adolescent will want to date nor should we try. Dating is a normal developmental stage in the life of an adolescent. If we recall our own youth, most of us will remember the stormy passions of early love affairs.

There are several generalizations about young adolescent dating, none of them quite true, that have evolved over the years. A brief examination of these issues may serve to lessen adult concerns.

1. *Adolescents begin dating at a young age because they are seeking the love they do not get at home.* Adolescents from all backgrounds and walks of life can be found in the young adolescent population who date.

2. *Puppy love is not real love and is meaningless.* I disagree with this, having spoken with young people who approach me on a daily basis for help in dealing with the pain of a broken relationship. Remember that adolescents live for the moment, and their emotions run high. To an adolescent who lives in the here and now, a broken heart is truly a broken heart! That said, the trauma of the ending will soon be forgotten, as long as unthinking adults do not resort to demeaning the relationship. In a few cases, this puppy love can last for years and decades. Since there are no laws governing adolescent relationships, we must remain flexible and open-minded.

3. *If adolescents date, they will automatically become sexually active.* Whether or not there is sexual activity in an adolescent relationship depends upon a number of variables. In any event, we have little control over sexual behaviors. What we do control is our ability to be a good role model and trust that previous teachings will prevent too-early sexual involvements.

4. *Not allowing an adolescent to date will prevent problems with the opposite sex.* Unfortunately, the only thing this will do is to force the adolescent to date in secret. Unless we spend twenty-four hours a day with the adolescent, we cannot enforce such a strict rule. Granted, some cultures prevent dating and arrange marriages, but this is certainly not the norm for our society. Keep in mind that adolescents today are far more sophisticated than we were at the same age, and they live in a fast-paced society that pushes sex and sexuality at them daily – it is unfair and impractical to never allow them to date.

5. *Expecting the worst and sharing this with the adolescent will scare him or her into acquiescence.* Probably the exact opposite is true as this story illustrates. Tammy was a lovely thirteen-year-old who had been involved with a fourteen-year-old boy for about a year. When she became pregnant, no one was particularly shocked. When Tammy went for adult counsel, the first question asked of her was "Why?" Tammy was unperturbed. She merely shrugged and said, "My mama was pregnant when she was my age, and she's been calling me a whore since I was about six." We need to realize that dating is normal and healthy, and that our attitude can have significant impact on the behavior of the adolescent.

6. *Open displays of affection should never be allowed.* What exactly does "open displays" mean? Holding hands? kissing? hugging? Naturally, many of these overt behaviors are inappropriate in certain locations, school being one of them. However, we need to consider whether we have the right to react strongly to two adolescents who are kissing or walking arm in arm in or around the home. These are outward signals of caring, and caring is an emotion we want to cultivate.

These suggestions are appropriate for young adolescents, aged thirteen to sixteen or seventeen. After that age, adolescents should be on their own with dating. At best, we can monitor the relationship and offer advice if it is sought. A great deal of flexibility comes into play now, and we must remember that today trust replaces what used to be structure.

"There is only one true happiness in life, to love and be loved."

George Sand

About Sexuality

Who do you turn to when you have questions related to sexual issues? Why? Do you think that sexual education courses should be a part of the school curriculum? Why? Why not?

Bev, aged fifteen:
"I talk to my friends or to this one adult that I trust. It's embarrassing to ask my parents. I definitely think sex ed is necessary at school because then you get to discuss things as a group. Sometimes I talk to Mrs. Wilson (a teacher) because I know she won't laugh and she will tell me the truth. I can trust her not to tell anyone else."

Although a few adolescents stated that they chose to discuss these matters with parents, the majority of respondents implied that it was easier to talk to a third party. Peers were the first choice, with single, significant adults – often teachers – second. Almost all adolescents were in favor of sex-ed classes at school since they allowed for frank discussions about sexual concerns with their peers in a safe environment. Many young people become interested in sex as young as ten or eleven years old and remain this way for many years. Adopting a heavy hand will not change this situation, but flexibility, open-mindedness, and a sense of humor will help. Consider the following examples of young adolescent statements about sex:

1. A young man in a sex-ed class was being introduced to the mysteries of conception. His only response was, "Cool!" When another student said something about that being the way in which all of us are conceived, the face of the young man fell and he murmured, "You mean my mom and dad did THAT? Gross!"

2. Shortly after a class on safe sex, two grade seven girls were overheard in the washroom. One girl said, "I don't know about you, but if I ever do it, I'm using a condiment." The other heartily agreed.

3. A parent asked the proverbial, "What did you learn in school today?" Her sixteen-year-old son, looking coy, answered, "Sex!" "Oh," replied the parent, "Are you still getting sex ed in high school?" "No," the young man laughed, "we had a substitute teacher, and Carmen and Jeff were in the closet all class."

Whether we like it or not, adolescents are aware of the opposite sex and of the nuances that accompany this awareness. The best thing that we teachers, parents, relatives, or friends can do is answer questions honestly and with a straight face. Younger adolescents are whizzes at double entendres, so be prepared. Older adolescents believe they know all that is necessary so discussions with them must be both subtle and factual. If an adolescent does not want to discuss a personal topic, respect his or her privacy and trust that she or he can handle it or seek help if necessary.

Experimentation

As much as we would like to change the situation, adolescents will experiment with sex. Given this reality, we must try to provide as much care, support, and acceptance as is possible. Certainly, we can discourage overt sexual behaviors and express concern about issues such as pregnancy and sexually transmitted diseases, but this must be done in a non-threatening way.

106

Some adults believe that adolescents most attracted to sexual experimentation are those who are emotionally deprived. While this may certainly be true in some cases, there are just as many adolescents from nurturing families that become involved in sexual activity. The point to be made is that the adult has little control in this situation, and certainly should not feel guilty if his or her child becomes sexually active. If you think your child is becoming sexually active, try to keep the adolescent among peers and make time alone in the home for the two difficult or impossible. If your child is sexually active, talk openly and encourage the use of devices that protect against pregnancy and sexual diseases without condemning the adolescent.

About Privacy

What are your thoughts about your need for privacy? Are there instances that bother you more than others?

Matthew, aged fifteen:
"I never get enough privacy. I could list one hundred examples when my privacy has been invaded. I really hate it. This is one thing about not being totally independent that bugs me the most. Like when my mom goes through my drawers. That isn't fair."

Of all questions listed in the questionnaire, this elicited the most vehement responses, leading me to believe that we don't realize how important a factor privacy is in the lives of adolescents. To this end, I have tried to identify why adolescents value privacy and ways in which we inadvertently trespass on this commodity.

One reason that might explain adolescents' overwhelming desire for privacy is the onset of puberty, which brings startling body changes that may both embarrass and confuse the young adolescent. In this instance, what the adolescent does not need is a nosy sibling or an interfering adult. What she or he does need is a great deal of privacy. Our off-hand remarks concerning new moustaches or growing breasts often disconcert the adolescent who is probably hoping that no one has noticed these changes.

Instead, what we might try to practise is structured support of the growing youth by providing unconditional approval as well as flexibility. As an example, your daughter comes in with a new haircut. You smile and wait for her to open the discussion. When she mentions the haircut, be supportive and non-judgmental despite the fact that you may not care for it a great deal.

A second reason for adolescents' desperate need for privacy is related to the emotional peaks and lows they experience. According to answers on the questionnaire, the right to "alone time" rates highly with adolescents of all ages. Like the issue of privacy, we often do not realize the adolescent need for their own space. Let us not be too quick, then, with our attempts to draw adolescents out and let us respect their right to be alone. You've noticed, no doubt, that part of this private time is spent in bed and in the bathroom. Where one bathroom is shared by many, this can become a major problem. If necessary, work out a schedule that provides everyone in the house with his or her own private time in the bathroom.

Another invasion of privacy involves reading an adolescent's diary. This, in fact, was often listed by adolescents as one of the things they disliked most about adults. On a television show where an adult audience was quizzed as to how many would read their adolescent child's diary, well over half responded in the positive. When questioned further, many admitted to the fact that not only would they read the diary, they would seek it out. Others mentioned regular room, desk, and drawer searches in the hopes of finding "something." Finally, some members of the audience felt that they had the right to read all correspondence addressed to their adolescent children. In extreme cases where an adolescent's room must be searched, it should be done only in the presence of the adolescent. In other cases, the adult should leave well enough alone. Invading the space and privacy of an adolescent will do little to promote good behavior. What it will do, however, is:

• tell the adolescent that you do not trust him or her,
• create open hostility,
• make you appear devious and untrustworthy,
• destroy adolescent faith in humanity,
• embarrass and upset the adolescent.

In all likelihood, these are not the results you seek. Take the scenario where you search a room and find an untoward item. Is the discovery worth the damage done to the adolescent-adult relationship? Just as I believe school lockers to be the private domain of the student, so too do I believe that a room or child's area in the home to be off-limits to adults. How can we expect young people to develop trust and integrity if this is the example we set for them? Adolescent privacy is a must!

A final situation cited by teens as a "horrible" action of adults is that of spying. This includes activities such as the ones below, all taken from questionnaire responses.

- They (parents) showed up at a party and pretended it was to see if I needed a ride, but I knew they were just spying on me. They always listen on the extension phone so me and the guys have to figure out a secret code.
- They listen to my messages on the answering machine and sometimes even erase them if they are from some guy they don't like.
- They always show up at the same place as I do just to see if I'm where I said I would be. Sometimes I feel like hiding so they think I'm not there.
- They open my mail, supposedly by "accident."
- They go through my belongings, my room, my closet, and my drawers.
- When I have a friend over, they try to listen to our conversations.

There is little I can add to this. Privacy is a right of all people, including adolescents. We cannot be flexible in our provision and respect of it if we want to build or maintain a healthy relationship with the adolescent.

About Money Matters

Do you think all adolescents should receive an allowance, and should it be based on specific responsibilities? What do you feel is one of the biggest concerns with the issue of allowance? How can an adolescent acquire money in other ways?

Kieran, aged thirteen:
"If I didn't get an allowance I wouldn't be able to do anything because I'd have to bug my mom for money and that would cause trouble. I really hate it when I have to ask over and over for my allowance. I have a friend who doesn't get an allowance so he tried to get a job. Now he just steals and sells stuff to get money."

The consensus of the adolescents was that the receipt of an allowance was important to their general well-being. They were not demanding or rude about the issue; they simply pointed out the necessity of having some spending money.

Not wishing to be redundant, I will merely remind readers that in most parts of North America there is little chance for today's adolescent, especially the younger adolescent, to be gainfully employed unless there is a family business. There are few jobs, and the ones that are available pay poorly and expect far too much in return. Consequently, any money the adolescent has must come from the home, hence the infamous allowance.

I agree with the adolescents when they say they have a right to some sort of allowance, the amount of which is naturally dependent upon the family income. There are two reasons for this: (1) an allowance can help an adolescent learn about money management, and (2) these are the years when the adolescent is expected to act much like an adult. This is an unrealistic expectation if the adolescent never has any money of his or her own. The allowance, however, must be structured. There are some general guidelines that may be helpful:

- The time and day of payment is consistent.
- The adolescent does not have to "nag" for the allowance.
- If the allowance is dependent upon completion of specific duties, these must be firmly established ahead of time, and are not subject to change unless agreed upon by both parties.
- An allowance should not be withheld for misbehavior. Other methods of discipline are far more effective.
- The adolescent has control over how she or he spends the money and should not be expected to purchase necessities (e.g., clothes, school supplies, toiletries) with the money. If the adolescent is responsible for the purchase of such items, the monies should be separate. Adolescents will learn money management when they find themselves without pocket money due to silly spending, rather than due to having to buy necessary items.

These suggestions are structured and leave little room for flexibility. The flexibility is in the amount of the allowance, the length of time between payments, and the expectations the adolescent is expected to fulfill. My preference is to make the allowance a separate entity, not dependent upon anything other than being a member of the family. For this reason, it can be kept relatively small, and an additional sum, not considered an allowance, can be made dependent upon such things as school attendance, grades, household chores, and so on. In this way, both structure and flexibility are encompassed, much in the way adults work within these two variables themselves. A specific, consistent sum is available for spending money; a variable amount may be available if earned.

The adult reaction to this may well be that this requires more money than is available. This is not necessarily so. Rather than giving a weekly allowance of $5.00, for example, give $2.50, and set aside the additional $2.50 as the flexible sum. In addition, it is also beneficial if adults can provide work-for-pay experiences for adolescents. There are always jobs around homes, schools, and institutions for which people are hired on an occasional basis. Why not hire an adolescent to clean the eves, repair the steps, paint the deck, or clean out a storage room? Again, this is not to say that certain responsibilities are not expected simply because one is a member of a group, but rather that they are responsibilities over and above the norm. Money matters are always going to be a concern for adolescents – they will never have enough. But then, do any of us? The best we can do is to make some money available consistently to them, and provide guidance in its use.

About Clothes

How much influence do you think adults should have over your choice of clothing?

Sophie, aged sixteen:
"None! If I am expected to act in a responsible way, then I should get to dress how I want to. I know that they (parents) pay for most of my clothes, but I wear them. What difference should it make as long as I'm not, you know, indecent or something? And nobody wants to be dressed different from everyone else! Some things are cool and some aren't. Why can't adults just accept that?"

The vast majority of the adolescents surveyed agreed that adults should have little or no influence on their manner of dress, other than to offer guidance when requested. However, many adolescents went on to state that they generally went along with adults' suggestions. The paradox here is, I think, explained by the manner in which we approach the situation. Again both flexibility and structure must interact. We are often dismayed by the way adolescents dress. I wonder how often adolescents hear the famous, "You can't wear *that* to school!" statement and ignore it. Relax! This is one area where peer pressure will win regardless of what you say or do. Instead of cringing at the outfit or hair, stop and reflect. What did you wear in your adolescence? Why did you wear it? The outfits put together by adolescents are innocent expressions of their growing independence. The key word here is innocent, for in truth, what harm do clothes cause? In fact, the flexible adult can actually enjoy the adolescent dress code. The following story emphasizes this point.

Alice, a gorgeous young adolescent with a beautiful figure, was to sing at a recital. She and her mother went shopping and found a dress and a matching hat that Alice could wear for the evening. According to Alice, her mother liked the dress because it "made her look innocent." Alice, however, felt that the dress looked "sexy." Both parties were happy. On the night of the ceremony, Alice decided not to wear the hat. Her mother, confused and dismayed, bit her tongue and said nothing. Alice was happy, and her younger sister wore the hat.

A mother whose daughter was graduating told me an interesting story. The daughter had decided to graduate as a "tree." She wore a lovely long green dress, and was planning to back-comb her long, dark hair until it stood on end about a foot from her head. Her mother wanted a photo of her daughter graduating so she asked her if she could take a picture before she did her hair. The picture was taken, the daughter then made a curious but attention-getting beehive of her beautiful hair, and everyone was happy. The mother in this example displayed both flexibility (do what you want) and structure (I'll take the photo first). The bottom line for those of us who must watch the disturbing parade of adolescent apparel, is "let them be." Unless the outfits are immoral (e.g., midriff tops on well-developed girls) smile, and say nothing. (Naturally, if the outfit is indecent, you may have to impose structure here, even at the expense of temporarily alienating the adolescent.)

Allow the adolescent to be cold in the winter (they never seem to wear jackets) and hot in the summer. They dress for appearance and not for practicality, but they will learn. We don't stop a young child from scribbling when he begins to experiment with crayons so we shouldn't stop an adolescent from experimenting with clothes. This is one area that is totally harmless and does not require adult interference. Be happy that you will have one less area with which to deal.

About Alcohol and Drug Abuse

Society considers alcohol and drug abuse by adolescents to be a concern. Do you agree or disagree? What suggestions do you have that would help society deal with this issue?

Willy, aged fifteen:
"It's not a concern for all of us, and society shouldn't blame all teenagers! Most of us are going to experiment and some kids do get into trouble with it. Then I think parents should deal with it by counselling and talking, not punishing. They (parents) can't watch us all of the time so all they can do is talk to us."

Joe, aged eighteen:
"One thing that is really stupid is even thinking about raising the legal drinking age. Then kids will just hide it more. It's hard to not drink if everyone else is drinking. I know some parents who have tried to make their kids stop hanging with kids who drink and smoke but all that does is cause lying. I guess since you're supposed to be an adult to do that stuff, if you mess up with it then you could be treated like an adult. . . fined or whatever."

As with all issues, there was a distinct change in attitude as the adolescent matured. Common to all ages, however, was the idea that the best intervention policy was counselling, open discussion between the parent and child, and understanding on the part of the parent.

Almost every adolescent will experiment with smoking, alcohol, or drugs at some point in his or her adolescence. While this may not be a pleasant thought for many of us, we need to distinguish between experimental or minor usage and actual misuse of a substance.

Experimentation

Adolescents are on a constant quest for knowledge and excitement. In addition, there is the pressure to conform. And we are all aware of the sweetness of the forbidden fruit. These factors contribute to the adolescents' experimentation in smoking, drinking, and drugs. Typically for younger adolescents, this represents nothing more than experimenting. If this is the case, we must not overreact. In fact, an overreaction at this time may ensure further investigation of the substances. I have used the adolescents' responses as the basis for the following suggestions:

- Let the adolescent know you are aware of the situation. Tell him or her this calmly and without judgment.
- Express concerns in succinct statements using the "I" method (e.g., I am worried because I feel that you are drinking too often. I know the problems that can cause).
- Avoid belaboring the point.
- Have some reading material on the subject available, but don't force the adolescent to read it.
- Have discussions in class that focus on the dangers of smoking, drinking, and drugs.
- Do not make the substances easily available to the adolescent.
- Be supportive and understanding if the adolescent has a bad experience with one or more of the substances.
- Have faith in the adolescent. Never assume she or he will partake of any substance other than in an experimental manner.
- Do not punish the adolescent for experimentation.
- Be a good role model – adolescents cited this as the most important thing an adult could do. This does not mean that you can never smoke or drink, but it should be done in moderation around adolescents.

Substance Abuse

What if the usage goes beyond experimentation? What if you suspect an adolescent of overuse or addiction? What if the adolescent is young, for example, seventeen or younger? To begin, we all know use of these substances by younger adolescents is illegal. More effective, according to adolescents, is our ability to assist the adolescent in finding professional help. There are teen-help groups and persons skilled in dealing with these problems in most communities. Some adolescents will refuse help – in these instances there is little you can do. The adolescent must be given the independence to suffer the consequences of his or her actions. Realize that the choice belongs to the adolescent and guilt, self-blame, or responsibility is not appropriate on your part. Similarly, for adolescents who are of legal age and who are substance abusers, there is little that can be done save being supportive and offering assistance if requested. The need for help must first be recognized and desired by the adolescent if it is to be effective.

I believe drug and alcohol abuse to be a more serious matter than smoking, although no doubt some of you would argue that point. Some adolescents do become addicted to smoking, most do not. If your child is one of the unfortunate ones, it's best to accept the reality but feel free to put limitations on it, more for your sake than his or hers. The statement that follows illustrates such limitations, as well as structure and flexibility that could not be frowned upon by even the most hostile adolescent.

"I realize I can't do anything about your smoking. I don't like it, but it's your decision. However, I do not want you smoking in the home, except in your room, and I would prefer that you not smoke in front of _____. Also, I will not lend or give you money to buy cigarettes."

I have used the following quote as a discussion starter with adolescents, and it may also prove useful in a home situation. In fact, a colleague has it printed on bright orange paper and attached to her 'fridge. She insists that it helped her sixteen-year-old son quit smoking.

"A custom loathsome to the eye, hateful to the nose, harmful to the brain, dangerous to the lungs, and in the black, stinking, fume thereof, nearest resembling the horrible stygian smoke of a pit that is bottomless."

James I

A Final Word

Some adults can talk to teens. They listen with their eyes, head, and heart, as well as their ears. They understand adolescent problems, admire their courage to fight for something in which they believe, and respect them as creators of the future. Even these adults, however, sometimes forget that today's adolescents act and react from an entirely different point of view.

Times change. A wonderful article included in a 1941 home economics book instructed women to, among other things:

- Meet your husband at the door, wearing a clean apron with a ribbon in your hair, with his slippers and newspaper in your hand.
- Make sure dinner is ready.
- Make sure the children are clean and quiet and waiting at the door to greet him. They are his little treasures and must look and act the part.

These criteria indicate how time alters our attitudes. The best way to modernize our views of adolescents and their thoughts, goals, and aspirations is to ask them. This is the premise on which this book is based. From this genesis – the questionnaire – suggestions have evolved that may help all adults to better communicate and interact with teenagers today. Perhaps, with a little assistance, more adults can be like the woman described by a fifteen-year-old girl.

> I can talk to Mrs _____. She doesn't make me feel embarrassed or dumb, or even expect me to be like she was at 15. She understands. And if she doesn't she says so and I try to explain. She is a totally cool adult. I want to be like her some day.

We can all be such significant adults. The process begins with understanding and ends with honest, open communication. Let's give adolescents our best efforts, one day at a time. They deserve no less nor do we.

The Questionnaire

Included on the following pages is a copy of the questionnaire I gave to more than three hundred students. Many of the findings arising from their responses to the questionnaire have been reported on in this book.

You may use the questionnaire to open doors of communication with your child or with students in your class. Given its length, I suggest that you ask adolescents to complete sections over a period of time. The questions, and the answers they elicit, may provide you with insights into today's adolescents and serve as a vehicle for increasing communication with the adolescents in your life.

Section A: Influences

Please number five of the following points in order of importance, one (1) being most important.

1. Good teacher traits:

____ intelligent

____ caring and warm-hearted

____ good disciplinarian

____ fair – treats all equally

____ attractive

____ young

____ good listener

____ friendly

____ interesting personality

____ dramatic (teaches with flair)

____ well-educated

____ knowledgeable

____ good role model

____ understanding

____ experienced

____ good sense of humor

____ good organizational skills

____ healthy and fit

2. Good parent or significant adult traits:

____ wealthy

____ intelligent

____ understanding

____ caring, affectionate

____ consistent, dependable

____ fair

____ attractive

____ good listener

____ forgiving

____ strict

____ good role model

____ interested in you and what you are doing

____ healthy and fit

3. Influences on you:

____ peers

____ teachers (in general)

____ specific teachers

____ parents

____ other adults (who _____)

____ relatives

____ television

____ books, newspapers, etc.

____ movies

____ music

____ older students

____ church

____ other organized social groups

____ team sports

____ activities out of school (e.g., dance lessons)

4. Things that bother you about being an adolescent:

____ being treated like a child
____ being treated like an adult
____ not enough free time
____ homework
____ too many rules at school
____ too many rules at home
____ no jobs available
____ too much time required by job
____ lack of money
____ being misunderstood by adults
____ being treated unfairly by adults
____ lack of emotional control
____ anxieties about the opposite sex
____ anxieties about yourself (e.g., appearance)
____ school

5. Things that adults do that annoy you:

____ drinking
____ yelling
____ not being where they say they will be
____ smoking
____ fighting
____ being phony
____ other (specify)

6. Things that are most important to you when dealing with the rules of society (e.g., family, school):

____ rules and consequences made clear
____ rules the same for all
____ rules established together (with you)
____ many small rules
____ many big rules
____ same rules for adults and teens
____ rules that are flexible
____ rules that are similar to those of peer group
____ rules that change with maturity
____ no rules at all
____ different rules for home and school
____ separate legal system for young offenders
____ few rules but with consistent consequences
____ no punishment for broken rules – warnings only
____ consistent consequences for all rules

7. Who do you feel gives you respect most of the time?

____ teachers in general
____ adults in general
____ specific teachers
____ parents
____ relatives
____ friends
____ peers in general
____ specific peers
____ police
____ store clerks
____ counsellor(s)
____ school principal(s)
____ other (name)

8. What adult actions give you the feeling that you are respected by them:

____ trusting you with money

____ talking to you as an equal (as opposed to a child)

____ listening to, and seriously considering, your ideas

____ telling you that you are respected

____ laughing with you

____ sharing general concerns (e.g., world problems) with you in a serious manner

____ being honest with you

____ trusting that you are honest with them – not doubting your word

____ giving you responsibilities and having faith that you can meet them without constant supervision

9. What adult behaviors/actions cause you to respect them:

____ having and keeping a job

____ rich

____ honest in word and action

____ sincere

____ fair (giving everyone an equal chance)

____ trusting as opposed to being suspicious

____ not being prejudiced

____ easygoing, relaxed most of the time

____ confident and sure of one's self

____ acting in an adult manner (as opposed to child-like)

____ friendly and caring

____ strong-willed

____ easily manipulated (letting you get your own way)

____ consistent and predictable

____ good role model

10. If you could change two things at school or home that would make your time there more enjoyable, what would they be:

____ personality of adult(s)

____ money available

____ physical set-up

____ number of rules and regulations

____ severity of rules and regulations

____ number of your responsibilities

____ type of your responsibilities

____ system of evaluation

____ behavior of adult(s)

Section B: Now and In Your Future

Please answer the following questions in point form.

1. What does "having more freedom" mean to you?

_____
_____
_____

2. Would you quit school right now? Why? Why not?

_____
_____
_____

3. What do you see in your future?

_____
_____
_____

4. Do you have a role model? If yes, who is your role model and why do you think of him or her in this way? If no, can you think of reasons why you do not have a role model?

_____
_____
_____

5. What makes you listen to some adults and not to others?

_____
_____
_____

6. If you could be any age you wanted, what age would you choose? Why?

_____
_____
_____

7. What makes you happy?

_____
_____
_____

8. What makes you unhappy?

_____
_____
_____

Section C: Discipline

1. What kind of discipline have you experienced? Was it successful? Why? Why not?

_____

_____

_____

_____

_____

2. Adolescent violence seems to be a big issue right now. What do you think can be done about it?

_____

_____

_____

_____

_____

3. What discipline would you suggest parents use with adolescents who:

(a) steal from parents

_____

_____

_____

_____

(b) shoplift

_____

_____

_____

_____

(c) use drugs or alcohol

_____

_____

_____

(d) use disrespectful words or actions

_____

_____

_____

_____

(e) break curfew

(f) refuse to co-operate at school

(g) refuse to co-operate at home

(h) lie

(i) leave homework unfinished more often than not

(j) fight

Section D: General Concerns

It is best to complete these questions singly, that is, one per session. They can be used as discussion openers or as essay starters.

1. Often people's marks tend to slip when they reach junior high. Has this happened to you? Why do you think this is a problem? Please suggest a way in which adults can help you prevent or overcome this problem.

2. How do you feel about homework? How can adults make this activity easier for you?

3. When people have little or no interest in the world around them and do not want to do anything to change their life, they are sometimes referred to as apathetic. As an example of apathy, some adolescents seem unmotivated and unwilling to put effort into school and/or home responsibilities. Do you fit this category? What do you think is the main problem affecting youth today?

4. What concerns, if any, do you have about the amount of independence you have?

5. Explain the importance of the time you spend with other adolescents.

6. At what age do you think adolescents should be allowed to go on unescorted dates? What restrictions do you think should be placed on dating?

7. Who do you turn to when you have questions related to sexual issues? Why? Do you think that sexual education courses should be a part of the school curriculum? Why? Why not?

8. What are your thoughts about your need for privacy? Are there instances that bother you more than others?

9. Do you think all adolescents should receive an allowance, and should it be based on specific responsibilities? What do you feel is one of the biggest concerns with the issue of allowance? How can an adolescent acquire money in other ways?

10. How much influence do you think adults should have over your choice of clothing?

11. Society considers alcohol and drug abuse by adolescents to be a concern. Do you agree or disagree? What suggestions to do you have that would help society deal with this issue?

Index

Abuse: 13, 14, 34, 84-85
  reporting, 33-34
Acceptance: 13, 14, 15
Accountability: 13, 14, 15, 57,
  67, 73-77
Adams, H.: 92
Advice: 23, 29, 42, 97, 105
Alcohol: 59, 67, 86, 113-115
Allowances: 76, 87, 98, 109-111
Anger: 67-70, 83-84, 86
Apathy: 94-97
Arendt, H.: 84
Arguments: 54, 68-70
Appreciation: 44, 45-47, 51, 61-62
Attention: 44, 45, 51-53, 68, 83
Attitude: 44, 47-51

Bacon, F: 102
Butler, S.: 90

Cars: 21, 82, 99
Child-Centred Approach: 12, 13,
  14-15
Clothing: 63, 79, 111-113
Communication: 14, 15, 17,
  28-42
  conferences, 36-38
  confidentiality, 33-34, 35-36
  non-verbal, 31, 33, 35, 38-40,
    41, 75, 85
  techniques for, 28-29
  timing, 30
  tips on, 31-34
  written, 34-36
Comparing: 27, 33
Consistency: 13, 18, 19, 25-27,
  41, 49, 74, 75-76, 93, 110

Criticism: 14, 49
  constructive, 37
Cruelty: 67, 86
Curfews: 54, 56, 67, 93

Dating: 103-105
Defiance: 67, 79, 100
Denial: 68
Deprivation: 44, 47, 86
Detentions: 55, 82-83
Discipline: 13, 15, 43, 44, 65-89
  corporal, 13, 83-84
  natural consequences, 13, 71,
    77, 78-81
  unnatural consequences, 77,
    81-85
Drugs: 65, 67, 86, 113-115

Evaluation: 27, 58, 74-75
  self-, 25, 58, 71, 72
Exams: 73, 74-75
Extra-Curricular Activities, 52,
  74

Favoritism: 25-26
Flexible Structure Approach:
  definition of, 14-15
Forgetfulness: 66, 78
Franklin, B.: 53
Friedenberg, E.: 11

Gangs: 16, 86, 87, 102
Goals: 14, 15, 44, 57-59
Grades: 90-91, 92
Grounding: 81-82

Homework: 56, 71, 75, 80, 82,
  92-94

Honesty: 14, 15, 17, 18, 19, 20, 24, 26, 29, 33, 41, 45, 76, 106
Hygiene: 36, 55, 60

Independence: 97-99
Indifference: 49
Irresponsibility: 79

James I: 115
Jobs: 46, 87, 110

Lates: 54-55, 67, 100-101
Limit Setting: 43-64
Lying: 19, 67

Militant Approach: 12, 13, 14-15
Money: 22, 63-64, 76, 87, 109-111

Nietzsche, F.: 28

Parties: 23, 98, 99, 101
Pearsall Smith, L.: 17
Peers: 14, 17, 52, 53, 80, 87, 91, 99-102, 105
Personal Space: 44, 59-60, 108
Pope, A.: 49
Power Struggles: 13, 69-70, 92
Privacy: 98, 106, 107-109
Promises: 26, 76-77

Reinforcement: 13, 14, 21, 43, 44, 52, 55, 58-59, 60-64, 73, 88, 93-94, 96, 97, 101, 111
examples of tangible, 62-63, 80
Rescuing: 15, 67, 70-73, 88, 97
Responsibilities: 17, 21, 55, 56, 76, 97, 102
Respect: 14, 15, 17-27, 31, 35, 44, 54, 56, 59, 71, 97, 98
Ritter, D.: 59
Rockefeller, J.D.: 43
Role Models: 14, 16, 17, 25, 27, 40-41, 104, 114
Rules: 12, 14, 15, 43-44, 53-57, 65, 74, 75-76
Russell, B.: 69

Saint Augustine: 99
Sand, G.: 105
Savile, G.: 68
School:
dropping out, 12, 91
truancy, 46, 100-101
Self-confidence:
of adolescents, 32, 34, 50, 69, 85, 95, 102
of adults, 18, 22, 24-25, 38, 41, 49
Sexuality: 104, 105-107
Shakespeare: 51, 100
Shaw, G.B.: 50
Silence: 22, 30, 32-33, 38, 49
Sleep-overs: 98
Smith, S.: 64
Smoking: 59, 113-115
Socrates: 65
Stowe, H.B.: 77
Swindoll, C.: 47

Tao Te Ching: 89
Telephone: 82, 99
Television: 82, 94
Theft: 16, 67, 72, 85, 86
Threats: 14, 56, 67
Time Outs: 67, 84
Time Sharing: 26, 52
Trollope, A.: 41
Trust: 14, 15, 17, 18, 19-24, 25, 27, 29, 33, 44, 54, 91, 97, 99, 109
Tutoring: 73, 80, 101-102

Vandalism: 16, 46, 65, 67, 80, 86
Violence: 16, 46, 65, 67, 85-86
reasons for, 86-87
dealing with, 87-89

Writing:
lines as a form of punishment, 83
notes, 34-36, 38, 61, 62

Yelling: 29, 67, 84